The Cultural Return

FLASHPOINTS

The series solicits books that consider literature beyond strictly national and disciplinary frameworks, distinguished both by their historical grounding and their theoretical and conceptual strength. We seek studies that engage theory without losing touch with history and work historically without falling into uncritical positivism. FlashPoints aims for a broad audience within the humanities and the social sciences concerned with moments of cultural emergence and transformation. In a Benjaminian mode, FlashPoints is interested in how literature contributes to forming new constellations of culture and history and in how such formations function critically and politically in the present. Available online at http://repositories.cdlib.org/ucpress.

Series Editors

Ali Behdad (Comparative Literature and English, UCLA)

Judith Butler (Rhetoric and Comparative Literature, UC Berkeley), Founding Editor

Edward Dimendberg (Film & Media Studies, UC Irvine), Coordinator

Catherine Gallagher (English, UC Berkeley), Founding Editor

Jody Greene (Literature, UC Santa Cruz)

Susan Gillman (Literature, UC Santa Cruz)

Richard Terdiman (Literature, UC Santa Cruz)

The Cultural Return

Susan Hegeman

UNIVERSITY OF CALIFORNIA PRESS
Berkeley · Los Angeles · London

University of California Press, one of the most distinguished university presses in the United States, enriches lives around the world by advancing scholarship in the humanities, social sciences, and natural sciences. Its activities are supported by the UC Press Foundation and by philanthropic contributions from individuals and institutions. For more information, visit www.ucpress.edu.

University of California Press
Berkeley and Los Angeles, California

University of California Press, Ltd.
London, England

Library of Congress Cataloging-in-Publication Data

Hegeman, Susan, 1964-
    The cultural return / Susan Hegeman.
        p. cm. – (Flash points ; 7)
    Includes bibliographical references and index.
    ISBN 978-0-520-26898-2 (pbk. : alk. paper)
        1. Culture–Study and teaching.   2. Popular culture–Study and teaching.
3. Mass media and culture.   4. Critical theory.   5. Culture and
globalization.   I. Title.
    HM623.H45 2012
    306.01–dc23

                                                                      2011026587

Manufactured in the United States of America

21   20   19   18   17   16   15   14   13   12
10   9   8   7   6   5   4   3   2   1

In keeping with a commitment to support environmentally responsible and sustainable printing practices, UC Press has printed this book on 50-pound Enterprise, a 30% post-consumer-waste, recycled, deinked fiber that is processed chlorine-free. It is acid-free and meets all ANSI/NISO (Z 39.48) requirements.

For Phil

Contents

Acknowledgments

This book arose out of an attempt to make sense of my local context, as an academic trained in the latter part of one century, and yet living in another. While I witnessed in one century a host of exciting possibilities brought about by the intellectual challenges of theory and interdisciplinarity, I found myself, in another, reckoning with forces that still evade comprehension: globalization, financialization, neoliberalism, and (perhaps most personally undergirding it all) what often feel like the final days of the American century's grand experiment in public higher education. As such, it has sometimes been difficult to write with much confidence about either my world or my place in it. Fortunately, I was able to share both my locality and the world of ideas with generous friends, mentors, and colleagues, all of whom I gratefully acknowledge here.

My first debts of gratitude go to conference and event organizers: Winfried Fluck and Thomas Claviez ("Theories of American Culture" at the John F. Kennedy Institut, Freie Universität, Berlin), Stanley Corkin (the Ropes Lecture Series at the University of Cincinnati), Fredric Jameson ("Anticipated Utopias: The Ethics and Politics of Collectivity" at Duke University), and Henrika Kuklick ("Histories of the Human Sciences: Different Disciplinary Perspectives" at the University of Pennsylvania). They kindly offered me the opportunity to elaborate on my earlier work on the concept of culture, which in turn led me to recognize an audience, sharpen my ideas, and find my polemic. Additionally, the annual Marxist Reading Group conferences at the University of Florida provided friendly, challenging, and inspiring venues throughout the writing process.

The following people gave me the invaluable gift of their time, reading drafts, sharing their work, and offering important support, advice, and insights: Alex Alberro, Matti Bunzl, Sarika Chandra, Kim Emery, Brad Evans, Richard G. Fox, Caren Irr, Sam Kimball, Sheryl Kroen, John Leavey, Barbara Mennel, Molly Mullin, Bruce Robbins, Barbara Herrnstein Smith, Trish Ventura, and the anonymous readers for the press. Other kind guides, facilitators, and co-conspirators include Rita Barnard, Ed Dimendberg, Pamela Gilbert, Peter Hitchcock, Kenneth Kidd, Carolyn Lesjak, David Leverenz, Peter Logan, Jane Love, Marc Manganaro, Chris Pavsek, Michael Rothberg, Malini Schueller, Rob Seguin, and Yasemin Yildiz. For sweet and savory little bits of local knowledge, I wish to thank Pam Kimball, Hannah Page, and Bob and Grace Thomson. And for providing me with mostly the right kinds of distractions, I thank Nadia and Owen, the Hegemans, the Hansons, the Wegners, and the Summer Institute and beach house families. Finally, and foremost, this book is a conversation with one particular interlocutor, who shares my world and keeps me thinking about utopian horizons. It is dedicated to Phil Wegner, alongside whom I write.

Introduction

In Jonathan Franzen's best-selling novel *The Corrections* (2001), one of
the plot lines involves the "failure" of an untenured cultural studies professor at a small northeastern college. Chip Lambert's downfall begins
when a bright student sabotages his class-capping exercise in the critical
analysis of an advertising campaign by interjecting, "Excuse me, but
that is just such bullshit."[1] The student, Melissa, complains that Chip
is trying to unload his own hatred of corporate capitalism on the students, when the ad in fact demonstrates the benefits of corporations;
in this case, the campaign for the software company centers on its
support of breast cancer research and awareness. Because this criticism
strikes Chip as somehow unanswerable, the whole semester's effort now
seems to him lost. Chip even feels compelled to ponder the rightness
of his former view that "criticizing a sick culture, even if the criticism
accomplished nothing, had always felt like useful work."[2] Indeed, he
begins to wonder if the culture of corporate and consumer capitalism
is really so "sick" after all—especially when bright young things like
Melissa seem so comfortable with it. Soon, he embarks on a disastrous
affair with Melissa, who involves him in plagiarism and illegal drug
use. For this, he gets fired from his job. To cover his living expenses
while he tries to get his life back together, Chip starts to sell off all his
academic books, saving for last his "beloved cultural historians and his
complete hardcover Arden Shakespeare."[3] Things only begin to look
up when he meets a shady Lithuanian entrepreneur who entangles him

in the complex new world of global klepto-capitalism. Together, they begin a scheme to bilk Western investors eager to claim their piece of beleaguered Lithuania's resources.

Of course, one wonders about how this little classroom controversy could have been sufficiently traumatic to provoke such a precipitous downslide. Melissa's comment is less trenchant than hostile, and Chip buckles at a confrontation that most experienced instructors would bat away with relative ease. (As to the merit of her point, not even Marx himself argued that capitalism was purely a force of evil in the world.) Indeed, we are given ample opportunity to psychologize Chip's rather sudden and irrational change of feelings about cultural studies, and also feminist and queer theory, as having something to do with his troubles with women. His embrace and rejection of cultural studies overlap with a long-term romance, recently ended, with a feminist graduate student. The specifics of his classroom crisis, a conflict over the relative harms of corporate media manipulation versus the merits of breast cancer research, also speak to his evident confusion over the sometimes competing pulls of feminism and cultural studies' putative anticapitalism. And finally, his dangerous relationship with the sexually free but happily capitalist Melissa decisively opens up a chasm between the liberation of desire and revolution, between critique and pleasure. Ultimately, at a kind of crisis point in which he turns his back on both feminism and anticapitalist critique, he is sold on going to Lithuania with the promise that the girls there are desperate to sexually service anyone for the promise of hard currency.

So we can at the very least say that Chip's relationship to cultural studies and his subsequent academic "failure" is hardly rational or dispassionate. He is ultimately a comic character, a fool. But what interests me here, nevertheless, is the trajectory Chip takes: from his pedantic embrace of cultural studies, to his (wounded) rejection of it, to his foray into pleasures that the critical project of cultural studies had seemed to denigrate, to a dicey salvation in the dangerous complexities of globalization. We may see this trajectory as a very thin allegory for the one that a lot of (former?) cultural studies scholars have been on in recent years. And while we might not identify with Chip's specific dilemmas, we may yet recognize, in comic form, some kinship with him in our frustrations over what might perhaps best be termed the exhaustion of cultural studies as a particular intellectual formation. If the hedonistic Melissa considers critique of the dominant society to be "bullshit," Chip's flip-side longing to locate sites of resistance and exteriority to it—in identity, desire, drugs, and so forth—seems both awkward and futile. And if an exciting new awareness of global realities seems to offer a kind of relief from this impasse, it is in the sense of a frank encounter with the real that cuts through these now predictable gestures. With globalization, the cultural studies problem of locating sites of resistance, spaces outside the system, finally seems nullified. What excites Chip is not just the prospect of seeing "a sweet little girl from the provinces get down on her knees" for dollars—the gritty experience of Lithuania as a peripheral player in a mean game of global exploitation—but his own complex implication in this situation, as the holder of those dollars.[4]

The historical context of this book is this moment of the apparent exhaustion of cultural studies as a central intellectual formation of the humanities and interpretive social sciences, and the concomitant struggle to identify the terms and methods by which to key these fields to an interpretation of our current social, political, economic, and geo-graphical situation. "Globalization," in this sense, is nothing more than shorthand for a general experience of historical change. Key events would include the post-1989 breakup of the Soviet bloc and the global supremacy of neoliberal doctrine. The instability arising from these dramatic changes has led, among other things, to unprecedented mass migrations of peoples—particularly from the underdeveloped South to the industrialized North—and the ascendancy of terrorism as a central political issue.

One significant consequence of these developments is a backlash against many of the fruits of the identitarian politics of the 1960s, including both theoretical and state-sanctioned multiculturalism. In the place of an older official rhetoric about the "recognition" of cultural minorities and multicultural constructions of national identities (as in Australia's 1982 *National Agenda for a Multicultural Society,* or in the United States' semiofficial construction as a "Nation of Nations") is a new, widespread emphasis in the former "first world" on the "civic integration" of immigrants and "race-blind" policies. But, as Christian Joppke argues, such changes can't be attributed to reactionary (racist, nationalist, xenophobic) backlash in any simple sense. As the compli-cated example of the Netherlands' Pim Fortuyn reminds us, such views are often buttressed with high-minded reference to state security, the rights of women and sexual minorities, and the core values of Western liberalism.[5] Supporting this official retreat from both identity politics and multiculturalism are an impressive number of academics, from across the political and disciplinary spectrum. In the United States, the academic repudiation of multiculturalism is reflected in the conservative "culture war" attacks on efforts to make disciplines more reflective of minority experiences. But it is also a stated position of many leftist and liberal scholars, who now balk, on any number of grounds, at the theoretical premises and politics of multiculturalism (some of these positions will be examined in the first chapter).

If responses to the current global situation have precipitated a retreat from multiculturalism, then we may see that it has in some senses unseated conventional poststructuralist thought as well, particularly its ban on theoretical totalization. As the authors of the Retort collective put it, "We take it the time is over when the mere mention of such categories [as 'capitalism' and 'primitive accumulation'] consigned one—in the hip academy, especially—irrevocably to the past. The past has become the present again: this is the mark of the moment we are trying to understand. (It is 'the end of Grand Narratives' and 'the trap of totalization' and 'the radical irreducibility of the political' which now seem like period items.)"[6] The Retort collective's vision of a rehabilitation of grand narratives seems generally accurate, but instead of a reinvigoration of those historicizing concepts of capitalism or primitive accumulation, what we have witnessed instead is a renewed interest in such key terms as "Enlightenment" and "Western civilization."[7]

In the academy, this return to grand narratives and universalism has disciplinary implications, leading to a renewal of interest in aesthetics, ethics, and even theology.[8] These interests are often combined, especially in the humanities, with methodological polemics against historicism, "content analysis," and "culturalism," and for a revival of such staples of disciplinary practice as literary formalism and cinephilia.[9] In this sense, such returns (and repudiations) are also couched in strongly institutional terms, as reactions to muddied and overreaching interdisciplinarity and as calls for renewed disciplinary clarity and coherence.[10] It is even argued that such a return to disciplinarity, close reading, and so forth is necessary in the face of increasingly urgent institutional imperatives to justify humanistic studies as an enterprise—as if ethics or aesthetics will finally serve as the conceptual talismans that will ward off shrinking budgets and programmatic cuts.[11]

In these accounts, the name for the "imperialist" interdisciplinary villain is usually cultural studies,[12] which—because it is often defined to broadly encompass the diverse energies of historicism and theory—claims neither a single method nor limits to its potential objects of inquiry. But cultural studies is also arrayed against these new trends in other ways. Whereas cultural studies foregrounded economic and political contextualization to the extent that the accusation of vulgar marketability always seemed to hover around the enterprise itself, aesthetics makes new claims for disinterestedness. And whereas cultural studies saw in laws and norms only disciplinary regimes, a return to ethics holds out the possibility of inquiry into broadly held human values.[13] To this overreaching, relativistic, anarchic, and hypocritically market-oriented cultural studies is opposed a newly sober, properly disciplined study of the good, the true, and the beautiful.

Attempts to historicize the various failures of cultural studies reach back into the 1990s, and similarly it is not hard to place such calls for a return to aesthetics and ethics within a zeitgeist.[14] As Alexander Alberro puts it, "In the face of the onslaught of catastrophes that have come to define our contemporary moment, it is not entirely surprising that writers who unequivocally reject the validity of critical artistic practices should call instead for a pathos-infused, humanist aesthetics."[15] Even more harshly, Alain Badiou criticizes the cooptation of intellectuals after the "collapse of revolutionary Marxism" by neoliberalism and the ideology of Western modernity: "Rather than seek out the terms of a new politics of collective liberation, they have, in sum, adopted as their own the principles of the established 'Western' order."[16] For Badiou, whatever the contemporary stimuli of such a return, it is fundamentally a reaction against the politics of the 1960s.

Hints of this reaction are also present in new calls for the return to the aesthetic, where beauty is aligned with a realm of pleasure neglected by the modernist (and political) emphasis on the sublime.[17] Or, somewhat more complexly, Chris Castiglia and Russ Castronovo have argued that cultural studies' crimes were against both pleasure and collective identity. They write, "Cultural studies, especially after its migration to U.S. institutional contexts, has debunked the essentialized identities and sanctioned intimacies at the base of most contemporary community formations, without supplying in their stead grounds for collective life that are affectively satisfying as well as theoretically plausible." According to them, the reascendance of the category of the aesthetic is a response to this putative failure in that it "traffics in affective sensations that promise—without necessarily providing—post-identity or non-normative forms of collectivism."[18]

Castiglia and Castronovo are ultimately interested in resolving the individualism of aesthetic experience with collectivity: that is, in renegotiating the relationship between aesthetics and politics. And in general, this is relatively typical of the new calls for considerations of the aesthetic, just as many observers and polemicists of the "turn to ethics" seem interested in bridging the gap between humanist universals and the particularities of identity and subjectivity.[19]

I am all for these kinds of projects. Indeed, the search for an intersection between aesthetics and politics, collective identity and private pleasure, universal and local values, or form and content for that matter is precisely the kind of dialectical project with which this book ultimately sides. But it is also important to emphasize that such a search for mediation is also antithetical to the polemics of those who would wish to limit literary scholarship to the study of the Literary, film scholarship to a pursuit of the Filmic, and humanities pedagogy in general to either an affective or an ethical encounter with beauty or pleasure.[20] So perhaps such reconsiderations of the relationship between aesthetics and politics are necessary now. But I also suspect that much of this project bears continuities with work in the humanities and interpretive social sciences that carry us back through the various sea changes of the last fifty years. My interest here is to interrogate why such calls for renovation feel necessary at this particular moment and—perhaps even more centrally—why they even feel like a change or break at all.

My approach to this question will be via the key concept of culture. For indeed, much of my skepticism about the originality of the project of considering the relationship between the aesthetic with the political is that this has long been a significant part of what used to be called cultural criticism, where the term "culture" has long stood in (in the words of Fredric Jameson) for precisely "the space of mediation between society or everyday life and art as such."[21] For Jameson, the relationship between art and culture is complexly dialectical: "The social pole of culture stands not only as content and raw material, it also offers the fundamental context in which art . . . has a genuine function to redeem and transfigure a fallen society."[22] So why the change in terminology? Why must the relationship between the aesthetic and the political go by another name besides "culture," and why must the study of this relationship be something other than, say, cultural studies or cultural criticism? Jameson argues that if "one feels a malaise in the face of this blurring of boundaries [between art and society], an anxiety about the indeterminacy in which it necessarily leaves the work of art itself, it then becomes crucial to break the link, to sever the dialectical movement, to challenge and philosophically discredit the concept of culture, in order to protect the space of art against further incursions of contamination."[23] "Culture's" problem is thus a disciplinary one. Jameson suggests that the move to conceptually uncouple art and culture both "restores art and the aesthetic to that sandbox in which [some feel] they rightly belong" and finally contains the myriad challenges and imperatives presented by the explosion of "theory" in the 1970s and 1980s.[24] So in this sense, the discrediting of the concept of culture is overdetermined. To its detractors culture is a signifier not only of the degradation of art and the slighting of form for an emphasis on content and context (history, ideology) but of the dangerous blurring of fields of knowledge and the disparate and disturbing interdisciplinary energies of theory itself.

In my view, the repudiation of the concept of culture—the turn away from the cultural turn of the 1980s and 1990s—is the transdisciplinary phenomenon that best represents our current perceived moment of intellectual rupture with the recent past. Often encompassing the various polemics for a renewed attention to aesthetics in art history, literature, and film studies, the turn away from culture also includes significant strains of argument within historical studies, philosophy, political science, and especially anthropology, one of culture's central disciplinary homes and yet the site of perhaps its most intense rejection.

Much of the criticism of culture, extending over the last twenty or so years, has been a more or less poststructuralist concern over the concept's connotations of historical and spatial fixity and its associations with eternal and hierarchical norms and standards. Whether "culture" is applied to a group of people or to a specific practice, it is often portrayed as overly rigid, ahistorical, reifying, sneakily polemical or evaluative, racist, normativizing, and elitist.[25] As I will show in chapter 1, this very project of pointing out the limitations of common usages of "culture" was a central gambit of the "cultural turn" of the 1980s and 1990s, in which the conceptual centrality of "culture"—largely redefined as hybrid, multivocal, migratory, and endlessly contested—was possible only after a thorough ground clearing of older conceptions of the term.[26] For others, in turn, this very poststructuralist revision of culture came in for critique—as itself a mystification of social, political, and economic considerations, or as a new kind of totalization, in which culture seemed to encompass anything and everything.[27]

In other words, one of the more constant features of the cultural turn was a lively debate about the meaning and utility of culture itself. This was especially true for anthropologists, among whom one may identify a veritable "writing against culture" genre and a countergenre of cultural defenders.[28] The moment of the cultural turn also produced a lively new interdisciplinary interest in the history of anthropology, especially the American tradition of Boasian anthropology, for which the concept of culture was so central.[29] Indeed, the development of such polemics within anthropology is unsurprising, as the discipline— especially in the United States—has long held a certain proprietary relationship to the concept. But by the late 1990s, the tone and direction of these debates over culture seem to have decisively turned. In 2003, Michael F. Brown wrote, succinctly, "In anthropology, which probably more than any other academic discipline gave culture high standing as an analytical category, culture's stock is at its lowest point in nearly a century."[30] And, as if to finally settle the cultural matter, Richard G. Fox and Barbara J. King have proposed that anthropologists not only get "beyond culture" but try to get "beyond culture *worry*" as well. Anthropology, they argue, can get along just fine without a consensual definition of this key concept.[31]

When the worry is over, then indeed it seems that a new moment in the discourse has emerged that does what so many of its polemicists have proposed: "forget culture," get "beyond culture," or at least make culture less vital to our discussions. Thus it is perhaps especially meaningful that sociologist Victoria E. Bonnell and historian Lynn Hunt (a key figure in the "new cultural history") proposed in a 1999 volume to probe "beyond the cultural *turn*."[32] Indeed, American studies scholar Michael Denning has recently historicized the cultural turn as something of the last gasp of the global moment of culture's centrality. For him, "culture" was the central problem in the "age of three worlds," that is, in the cold war era and the moment of postcolonial liberation struggles. Given that this era is now decisively over and our attention has turned to the global context of the present, culture is for him also a thing of the past.[33]

Denning's point is compelling and will require further comment in chapter 3. But for now we might also note that his book *Culture in the Age of Three Worlds*, so inflected by world systems analysis, is exemplary of the disciplinary context of the turn away from the cultural turn. For another way to look at the matter is to see the cultural turn as a particular moment in the history of interdisciplinary contact between the humanities and the social sciences. Whereas British cultural studies was most deeply indebted to sociology as its major social scientific disciplinary influence, in the United States the central social scientific other was anthropology. It was Clifford Geertz who inspired new historicism and the new cultural history, thus famously (and for many other anthropologists, frustratingly) becoming the anthropologist that all the historians and literary scholars read.[34] But the new ethnic studies of the 1970s and 1980s were also largely the products, in organization and often in personnel, of area studies, which had strong historical connections to anthropology. Meanwhile, through an emphasis on fieldwork, cultural studies turned to anthropology as a kindred discipline. And ultimately, anthropology came up and met the humanities with its own culturalist turn, represented by the controversial "reflexive" anthropology, which—to the consternation of anthropologists more comfortable with "harder" social scientific approaches—incorporated the poststructuralist theory then central to cutting-edge work in the humanities. Anthropology, in this moment, became significantly textual, while many scholars in the humanities became enticed by fieldwork and ethnography.[35] The repudiation of the cultural turn, then, marks the end as well of this particular interdisciplinary moment, or rather a shift in the interdisciplinary interlocutor of the humanities from anthropology to other fields—perhaps fields better prepared to help us understand globalization—such as geography and world systems analysis.

Yet for all this significant reshuffling of the interdisciplines, culture doesn't quite seem vanquished. Anthropologist Nicholas Dirks—still working in the interstices of the humanities and the social sciences—offers a compelling spectral vision of "culture" "in near ruins." Organized around a fundamental "lack" (of, among other things, a precise consensual meaning), culture haunts us as "the impossible object of our critical conscience."[36] For clearly, "culture" has not so much gone away as it has diffused into the woodwork of myriad discursive sites.

As everyone since Raymond Williams and Kroeber and Kluckhohn has reminded us, "culture" has a long and complex history that does not parse into easy conceptual units or ideological camps.[37] There are any number of strains of cultural theory that we may find outmoded, inflexible, or even politically or personally repugnant. But I find the various calls get rid of culture, to expunge it from our critical vocabularies, if taken literally, to be nonsensical, as if one could wave away what are now several hundreds of years of intellectual history—or indeed expel concepts into some kind of linguistic limbo. Such a project seems to me to presuppose a fantasy of purely transparent communication or, worse, an idealism in which concepts somehow operate independently of the contexts in which they are deployed. Or perhaps the business of getting beyond culture is a mere rhetorical gambit after all. If that is the case, then the discourse just seems curiously detached. For, while scholars articulate complex reasons for disliking "culture," the popular and political rhetoric of culture becomes more complex and strident by the day.

A few examples of "culture's" popular ubiquity should suffice. A quick word search in the Lexis-Nexis database of U.S. case law will reveal a wealth of usages of "culture," some working in the familiar registers of multiculturalism (is it, for example, a matter of housing discrimination if a tenant doesn't want to share an apartment with a person of a certain "cultural" background?) and others referring to specific national contexts (say, in speaking of an employee who was hired for her knowledge of something called "Japanese culture"). Then there is the odd reference to "drug culture." But most of the references will pertain to this or that subset of "corporate culture": boardroom culture, or the culture of a particular firm or industry, as in the phrases "corporate culture of ageist discrimination" or "an ingrained culture of fraudulent practices." At my university, differences in "departmental cultures" are sometimes invoked to explain the variety of attitudes across the campus regarding administrative initiatives, hiring, tenuring, interunit cooperation, and so forth. A wave of tragedies among MIT students several years ago provoked concern that there was a campus-wide "culture of suicide." Meanwhile, Japan's "culture of stoicism" apparently masks the problem of mental illness in that country, and advertisers consider the pros and cons of marketing to a "global teen culture."[38] But these various usages are mere rhetorical trivia compared to the increasing clamor, globally, for cultural identity, recognition, and autonomy. Clearly, we are existing in a moment when the basic conditions of accelerated cultural mobility and exchange are producing an increasingly self-conscious perception among many peoples of their having something called a "culture." As Marshall Sahlins has quipped, "Pretty soon everyone will have a culture; only the anthropologists will doubt it."[39]

These various and polyglot vernacular usages could, of course, suggest the very problem with "culture" as a technical term. If it possesses all these meanings, has it not lost its efficacy for specialized discourse? Or is not the very recognition that one has a culture a sign of its debasement—a measure, in fact, of its reification and potential commodification? This is an interesting, and inevitable, perspective, but it also suggests an inverse proposition: If "culture" as a term is so widely and publicly embraced, why should that imply only a degradation of meaning? Why, instead, isn't this the appropriate moment for scholarly engagement with a public that seems to at least think it understands what it means to have a culture, and indeed to think culturally? A cognate of Sahlins's point is that apparently only academics seem right now to find culture unimportant and suspect.

But this is not just an issue of academic versus vernacular rhetoric, for "culture" has become a particularly politically charged term in recent public debate. We are repeatedly informed these days that we are in the middle of a hot "culture war," a phrase all but owned by the likes of conservative television personality Bill O'Reilly.[40] Far broader than the largely academic 1990s battle over canons and curricula, this current war is a more all-encompassing affair between those who claim to hold traditional (often religiously inspired or mandated) values and beliefs and those on the "cultural left," who are seen as promulgators of new, "politically correct" attitudes and mores.[41] The phrases "culture of life" and "culture of death," first articulated in Pope John Paul II's 1995 encyclical *Evangelium Vitae,* have now become commonplace in the political rhetoric of the American Right. For these American "culture warriors," as for the late pope, a "culture of death" encompasses not only such specific flashpoints as abortion, stem cell research, euthanasia, and homosexuality but the legacy of the Enlightenment itself: social secularism, scientific inquiry, and the ethics and politics of human rights and liberties.[42]

So our problem is not just that the public has taken a shine to culture but that an impressive number of political and social conservatives and reactionaries currently seem enamored of the idea. Drawing upon the academic imprimaturs of cultural determinists like Thomas Sowell and Samuel Huntington, conservatives have now successfully deployed culture to explain a host of ills and issues from poverty and teenage motherhood to murder.[43] Which is to say that, from this rightward perspective, culture and cultural differences have taken the place of other explanatory apparatuses that emphasize oppression or injustice, especially racial or gender oppression and discrimination; historical injustices such as colonialism and imperialism; and the current global context of economic exploitation.[44]

This development is perhaps particularly disturbing for those trained within the liberal habitus of the social sciences, for whom culture figures prominently within heroic stories of disciplinary founders who used the culture concept to publicly debunk racism and other forms of social injustice grounded on assertions of innate or biological human differences.[45] While one might suggest that these stories of culture's success in sweeping away Social Darwinism (or racism!) were always simplistic, the sense that a classic rhetorical tool of liberal discourse is now being appropriated by the Right is nevertheless both disorienting and dismaying. In this sense, culture joins a number of other liberal and left ideas and strategies that have been skillfully repackaged for the furtherance of conservative interests.[46] This is notoriously the case with "political correctness," once an accusation of excessive dogmatism used among political leftists, which has now been successfully coopted to pejoratively label just about any expression of liberal sentiment. Currently, we may also see clever manipulations of such basic liberal ideas as "diversity," "representation," "balance," and even "fairness." Thus the promoters of creationism urge the teaching of "intelligent design" alongside Darwinian evolution as a responsible example of "teaching the conflicts"—an idea that Gerald Graff among others had earlier offered as an ethical *liberal* approach to engaging students with the positions of various academic controversies. Or, to take a more obvious example, we have seen how the rhetoric of affirmative action has been used against itself, as figures like Clarence Thomas, Alberto Gonzales, or Condoleeza Rice have been held up as unassailable exemplars of representativeness and inclusion. Under the slogan of "intellectual diversity," David Horowitz (founder of the Orwellian Students for Academic Freedom) has attempted to extend the multicultural goals of cultural sensitivity and tolerance to the protection of political and social conservatives, whom he asserts to be an oppressed minority on college campuses.[47] Indeed, even Samuel Huntington's famous "clash of civilizations" thesis partakes of this interesting stratagem of playing the oppressed cultural minority: while for him the West is still the bearer of a unique civilizational mission to the world, "Western civilization" is not only distinctive but rather fragile, requiring protection and nurturance for its survival.[48] But these irritating rhetorical games are nothing compared to more pernicious transitions in which, for example, the New Right in Britain strategically deployed the cultural rhetoric of leftist cultural studies, anthropology, and antiracist politics to formulate a new rhetoric of anti-immigrant nationalism.[49] Or, as Alice O'Connor has argued, the very cultural accounts of poverty formulated decades ago as part of agendas of radical social transformation have become the basis for conservative and neoliberal arguments for dismantling the welfare state.[50]

What does it mean that "culture," undeniably a central term of a left-leaning academic discourse in previous decades, has now become accessible to this kind of manipulation? Many of the writers against culture would use such examples to argue both that there is something inherent in the idea of culture that is only now exposed in such conservative deployments and that such usages are signs of the concept's necessary obsolescence. Indeed, others have gone so far as to suggest that those who have deployed cultural theory to honorable ends were from the beginning dupes of the powerful—or worse, their willing agents—distracted from the real issues of economic disparity, violence, and injustice characteristic of our global moment. In his dystopian picture of a new world order run by an Inner Party of the cosmopolitan "super-rich," Richard Rorty argued that "cultural" matters would be revealed to be what they always in a sense were: the political bread and circuses of interethnic conflict and moral panic that keep the "proles" distracted from basic issues of economic inequity.[51]

But this book takes another tack. To those impressed by arguments such as Rorty's, I would ask whether we must really see the cultural field as rigidly distinct from issues of economic inequality. Is the separation, if it exists, really as final and fatal as he suggests? Analytically, I don't believe it is: When are interethnic conflicts not also inflected with issues of economic exploitation and subordination? But rhetorically, I believe we are in danger of ceding the domain of culture to those who we already know have a deliberately limiting understanding of it. In other words, we need not only to take back the terms of public debate, of which I believe "culture" remains an indisputable part, but to do an overall better job even among ourselves in defining and defending the ground of culture.[52] In this respect, I agree with Peter J. Richerson and Robert Boyd, who have recently written, "Frankly, we think that the defenders of culture have grown complacent and lazy. Secure in the moral conviction that only people with evil intentions subscribe to racist notions like genetic explanations for human behavioral differences, or capitalist ones like rational choice, anthropologists, sociologists, and historians have neglected their knitting."[53] To this list, I would only add that literary and cultural studies scholars also have something to offer in this venture, though they are too often caricatured in novels like *The Corrections,* and among many scholars, as the authors of culture's woes.

My goal here is to examine the field of cultural analysis to the end of reasserting the vitality of cultural discourse. As such, I'm also taking a page from Clifford Geertz and his magisterial *The Interpretation of Cultures:* I'm interested not so much in an ontological understanding of culture as in its deployment, its effects, its utility.[54] Indeed, though I do rehearse and systematize some of the important arguments against culture in our current moment (this is largely the work of chapter 1), I am centrally interested in considering what it would mean to develop a positive and socially progressive idea of culture—one that might be not only acceptable to academics but more popularly useful and engaging.

Here I perhaps reveal that the populist impulses so central to cultural studies have stuck with me. But other important traditions of "culture" can similarly serve as examples of mediating points between scholarly research and popular discourses on society. Most important to me, and haunting this study in ways that are probably obvious, are the cultural criticism of Raymond Williams and the Boasian school of American anthropology. Boas and his students theorized "culture" in the context of a very important and in its day quite challenging point that went to the heart of both nineteenth-century racial theory and romantic nationalism: that there is no necessary relationship or spatial contiguity between nation-states, languages, races, and cultures. In other words, if a group of people with a presumably common genetic makeup speak a particular language, practice a particular set of customs, and live in a particular location, this is not a product of some natural affinity between blood, tongue, and soil but the deeply contingent result of an often complex history that includes factors such as migration, invasion, trading relationships, political alliances, and so forth. While this may seem like common sense to us now, the radicality of this point in its context is not to be underestimated. It offered a way for Boas and his students to conceive of factual refutations to several powerful varieties of nationalist thought, which, in their different forms, posited the coextensiveness of the nation with the spatial spread of a race or ethnicity, culture, and/or language.[55] It also countered many of the premises of scientific racism and a good deal of philological and historical thinking. It allowed antiracist anthropologists, and those influenced by them, including the important African American intellectual W. E. B. Du Bois, to make some very powerful statements about racial politics, and it opened up the space for providing more complex and historically informed understandings of how migrations and contact between peoples influenced custom, language, religion, and much else.[56]

Culture was particularly effective against biologically based conceptions of difference such as race precisely because it was historically contingent. It could therefore be subject to change and even manipulation. Thus, for example, when Margaret Mead, in *Coming of Age in Samoa* (1926), compared American views of adolescence with a Samoan counterexample to show how the very category of "adolescence" was a peculiarly Western invention—and a peculiarly American site of concern—the payoff was not simply the exercise in cultural relativism but the lesson that the biology of adolescence was no more destiny than was the biology of race. If adolescence, or differences of race and gender, could be shown to be cultural, then *things could be otherwise.*[57] The cultural was the site of that which was malleable, subject to the processes of history and contact, but most of all subject to change through education—to enlightenment. Ultimately, it is against such a utopian project where an unlikely group of players tend to agree: the conservative culture warriors, battling back the Enlightenment; academic critics of the culture concept, sometimes battling for it; and even popular wielders of the discourse of culture. For all of these, it seems, share a suspicion of such transformative possibilities for and through culture—of what Jameson called culture's "genuine function to redeem and transfigure a fallen society."[58]

Though academic cultural discourse certainly acknowledges the elements of change, creativity, performance, and improvisation in culture, it is generally (and appropriately) wary of the suggestion of social engineering that was implicit in some earlier discussions of culture; culture may change, but it is not now generally regarded as subject to controllable or predictable change. Meanwhile, in the realm of popular usages, culture is often invoked as something very close to the idea of "heritage," something that ought to be preserved and protected, passed down from generation to generation, or to connote something that is lamentably unchangeable: we do this or that because it is part of our culture. Certainly, this is a nuance of the examples I cited regarding "corporate culture," "departmental culture," and "drug culture": such usages are meant to suggest a more or less intractable pattern of group behavior. But what is equally striking to me is that as "culture" thus seems increasingly *less* connotative of alteration, the *biological* seems, in an odd reversal, increasingly to be a site of plasticity and change. This is, of course, in the context of new technologies such as gene therapy, cloning, assisted reproductive technologies, sex reassignment and cosmetic surgeries, and so forth. And this sense of immutability comports perfectly with the views of the culture warriors on the right, who if anything see such change as precisely the ground upon which to wage battle.

But this possible convergence of views of culture hardly supports academics' quietism on the topic of culture. Indeed, if the Boasian project seems to have been seriously questioned on the grounds of culture's centrality to social change, then one must also note certain significant victories. Though it is absurd to suggest some kind of wholesale Boasian triumph over the concept of race, it doesn't seem intemperate to claim that the fundamental Boasian proposition about the contingent relationship between race, language, culture, and nationality has been widely accepted. There is, certainly, a whole, often ugly history to be written on the way these conceptual frames of language, race, nation, and culture have been linked and unlinked, mapped upon and over one another and then spatially uncoupled—the violence of which has been dramatically revealed in recent decades in places such as Israel, West Africa, the Balkans, and the former Soviet Republics. In the United States we see traces of these linkages in the context of anti-immigration and "English-only" movements and various eruptions of the "culture wars" over the content and meaning of American history and culture. Yet despite these struggles, very few in the United States would accede to the idea that the United States as a nation is coextensive with *one* culture, *one* race, or even one language. Other indicators also point to an even more general delinking of culture or race from nationality, as, for example, in the international trend in immigration law, in which citizenship is increasingly assigned according to the location of one's birth rather than based on the citizenship of one's parents.[59] Whether everyone finds this state of affairs agreeable is another issue, but I think the very presence of various racist and ultranationalist rearguard actions only strengthens my view that that the traditional linking of culture, race, and language to the political entity of the nation has significantly broken down. This breakdown also helps explain the proliferation of some of the vernacular usages of "culture" that I mentioned—drug cultures, departmental cultures, corporate cultures—all of which obviously refer to collectivities that are in no way aggregated on the basis of race, language, or nationality. It also explains the elaboration of theological, environmentalist, and other usages of the idea of culture that transcend locality and particularity. Indeed, as I will discuss in my final chapter, "culture" is now firmly ensconced within international law, where it is deployed in, among other contexts, international definitions of human rights.

All of this is simply to say that there is still a useful and informative relationship between vernacular and technical usages of terms such as culture and that therefore the academic and disciplinary calls to get beyond culture also have consequences in our more public discussions. When we dispense with culture, assert its meaninglessness and inutility, we are also assenting to the advertisers and propagandists, who will then happily shape the discourse and finally the terms of debate. Or we concede to scholars like Samuel Huntington, who yokes his highly deterministic notion of culture to ideologies of American imperial prowess and perpetual war.

Yet arguing for a return to culture also entails a due sense of humility—humility, I would suggest, that comes in large part from working in a ground once cleared by poststructuralist theory. We now all know and understand the limits of certain gestures of identity construction; of fixing borders and delimiting fields; of "bad" totalization. So I'm certainly not interested here in offering a singular purified conception of culture that promises to dispense with these challenges. Rather, my emphasis is on the historical specificity of usages of culture, and insofar as I am interested in "return," it is in retaining certain modes of thought that I argue are integral to cultural discourse. Culture forces us to think about the relationship of the individual to the collectivity and collectivities of different kinds to each other; about the form and functions of collectivities; and ultimately about the relationship between the worlds we inhabit and our loftiest hopes. Very few concepts, I think, help us to think about these things. And very few concepts force us into the embarrassments of recognizing the limits of our own impoverished imaginations.

This book is organized both as a series of discrete chapters on related topics and as a long essay on a definition of culture as dialectically intertwined with the concept of modernity. This argument, summarized at the beginning of chapter 6, is elaborated throughout, but especially at the end of chapter 1 and in chapter 5. The more specific argument of chapter 1 involves a systematic look at some of the arguments against "culture" from several disciplinary positions, especially anthropology and literary studies, beginning in the moment of the cultural turn. There I challenge a series of often mutually self-canceling complaints against the term and its usage, especially arguments that it is a reification of identity; that it is a meaningless or ungrounded abstraction; or that it is tied to conservative and/or objectionable ideas like race and religion. In the place of these critiques, I offer a characterization of the rhetorical field of culture that portrays the term as fundamentally dialectical, mediating between a series of historically specific contradictions, such as those obtaining between the individual and the totality (the collective, the social, the environment, the biological), the local and the global, the contingent and the structural, the aesthetic and the quotidian, or the present and the (desired) future. As a concept centrally invested in the process of describing "the wholeness of history," culture has long served as the site where thinkers have imaginatively grappled with the shattering experience of modernity.

Even while offering a theoretical treatment of a dialectical culture, chapter 1 attempts to show that the contradictions within and around which the term works are historically specific. In chapter 2, I extend this point by making the case that one well-known deployment of the culture concept, "mass culture," needs to be resituated within a specific historical context. While critics have often addressed mass culture as a largely decontextualized matter of taste and consumption, I argue that it is best relegated to the decades preceding World War II, when several specific historical factors converged: new techniques of mass communication (especially radio) and the existence of vital public spaces that accommodated and even encouraged the assembly of literal *masses* of people in one place. That this historical context no longer resonates with us is also historicizable, the product of the postwar privatization of social space. Ultimately, I offer this as an example of the work that must be undertaken to rehistoricize various meanings of the concept of culture and thus make it seem less as if "culture" were everything.

The subsequent chapter then turns to the cold war era (postwar to the 1990s) to historicize the cultural turn itself. In what sense, and in what context, did "culture" actually seem like the central, crucial, object of study, to the extent that it was possible for some to say that "everything" was cultural, or indeed for whole departments—nay, colleges— of scholars to assert that they *all* did "cultural studies"? I show how "culture" became a term that seemed to offer a conceptual resolution to central conflicts of the period, from the new political mandates arising from postfascism and the cold war to respect cultural difference in the context of universal norms of human rights to the post-1968 problem of resolving new assertions of political identity with postidentitarian political and philosophical positions.

Chapter 4 addresses the problem of borders—especially the problem of national borders and, as a kind of analogy, the problem of disciplinary borders. In particular, I compare the "getting rid of culture" position in anthropology to recent anxieties in the field of American studies over another concept: that of "America" itself. Through this comparison, such calls for this kind of conceptual renovation are shown to have some characteristic contours. The anti-"culture" and anti-"America" positions both respond to similar concerns about nationalist biases—an issue of particular relevance in the context of current global politics. But they also respond to more affective concerns of scholars in American studies and in anthropology, who see themselves as politically and socially progressive inheritors of outmoded and problematic disciplinary histories. While such moves to jettison key concepts may in fact be undesirable or even impossible, they nevertheless serve to reinforce the habitus of specific disciplines. The work of this chapter is to rethink disciplinary histories to make such rhetorical moves both less powerful and less affectively appealing.

Chapter 5 addresses one interdisciplinary attempt to develop a conceptual frame for coming to terms with our current global realities: the turn toward religion. Religion is held to surpass culture as a site of analysis in that it seems to more adequately address the problem of individuals' commitments to communities and forms of behavior. Culture, in this view, is trivial—mere adherence to form and custom— whereas religion and *belief* explain the motivations of, say, the suicide bomber. Ultimately, I see this distinction between culture and belief as being overdrawn. But what interests me more here is the implicit deployment of a narrative of modernity and its others, where belief is implicitly a property of those still outside modernity and Enlightenment. I argue for a wholesale rejection of this romantic fantasy, and ultimately for a more complex conceptualization of culture's relationship to modernity that will allow us to apprehend the significant changes of our current moment.

One of these changes is the increasingly vocal call on the part of many national minorities and indigenous groups for cultural recognition. This, in turn, goes hand in hand with the emergence of an international regime that has enshrined cultural recognition as a central aspect of human rights. In the final chapter, I not only argue for the ethical and intellectual necessity of acknowledging local articulations of culture but consider the ways that this development reflects our current state of global denationalization. Indeed, culture represents a central term for articulating a number of important changing features of contemporary life, including the constitution of group identity, the nature of political authority, and the construction of such fundamental ideas as rights and property. As such, I hold, it remains a concept that best allows us to imagine new and other arrangements and ways of being for the future.

Which brings me back to Chip of *The Corrections*. Ultimately, his experience as a global adventurer does teach him a few things. He learns, for starters, that the Lithuanian prostitutes are not desperate young girls but adult women with complicated lives who see servicing him as a rather boring job. He learns that he and his friend are in over their heads, playing in a world that is both deeply politically unstable and controlled by forces far more powerful than they. He learns, in other words, about the interplay of power relations in a local context deeply enmeshed in global struggles. Chip returns home broke and scared, eventually to become support and caretaker for his disabled and emotionally repressed father. Ultimately, Chip's is also a cultural return, not only in that he relocates in his natal American Midwest—a locale that has also suffered the ill effects of globalization and financialization—but in that he finally accepts the idea that resistance lies not in a space elsewhere but rather in a return to his own past.

CHAPTER I

Cultural Discontents

The documents having now piled up on its putative grave, what are the central arguments against the culture concept? The answer to this question is often shot through with the specificities of the disciplines from which the writer emerges, so that the anthropologist's concerns are never quite the same as the literary critic's, the cultural studies scholar's, the evolutionary psychologist's, the historian's, or the political scientist's. I'll return to the issue of disciplinarity later. But here, my effort is to be as synoptic as possible, in order both to systematize the often self-contradictory claims made against culture and to offer some account of how these arguments reflect larger concerns and trends.

So to begin, I offer the following list of common complaints against culture:

1. Culture is reified: it demarcates solid boundaries of belonging, without regard to complex processes of contact, creativity, and change.

2. There is no such thing as culture: its meaning is imprecise and it is insufficiently referential of the "real" structures of human existence.

3. "Culture" is just a sneaky word for "race," a scientifically outmoded and politically objectionable concept.

4. Culture is politically conservative.

5. Culture is substitute religion.

These issues are sometimes clearly related, as in the conjoined complaints that culture is conservative and that it represents covert religious thinking. Similarly, the idea that culture is just another way of demarcating race emerges from the idea that it is an abstract nothing: if "culture" means anything at all, then what it connotes simply recapitulates another problematic abstraction. At other times, what is striking is these critiques' significant opposition to each other. Thus the concern that culture is too easily reified, that it implies solid boundaries and demarcations of inclusion and exclusion that simply don't exist, is exactly the inverse of the worry that there is no such thing as culture, that it is a meaningless abstraction. It is in these sites of opposition that we see the real contours of the debate over culture since the cultural turn.

1. CULTURE IS REIFIED

In *The Predicament of Culture* (1988), a key document of the "cultural turn," James Clifford made an interesting prediction:

> An intellectual historian of the year 2010, if such a person is imaginable, may . . . look back on the first two-thirds of our century and observe that this was a time when Western intellectuals were preoccupied with grounds of meaning and identity they called "culture" and "language" (much the way we now look at the nineteenth century and perceive there a problematic concern with evolutionary "history" and "progress"). I think we are seeing signs that the privilege given to natural languages and, as it were, natural cultures, is dissolving. These objects and epistemological grounds are now appearing as constructs, achieved fictions, containing and domesticating heteroglossia. In a world with too many voices speaking all at once, a world where syncretism and parodic invention are becoming the rule, not the exception, an urban, multinational world of institutional transience—where American clothes made in Korea are worn by young people in Russia, where everyone's "roots" are in some degree cut—in such a world it becomes increasingly difficult to attach human identity and meaning to a coherent "culture" or "language."[1]

Clifford nicely captures several things here. First, he historicizes a certain concept of culture, which he calls "natural culture," as the product of a particular moment and equally shows how inadequate such a concept is for conceptualizing a present characterized by what everyone would soon be calling "globalization." Yet despite his relegation of this culture to the past, Clifford's statement of another, more heteroglossic, mobile, and syncretic cultural alternative would become a central preoccupation of the cultural turn. So an interesting feature of the cultural turn is precisely "culture's" centrality as the frame of reference *in the face of* a widely held view that the term in its received meaning ("natural culture") is either inadequate to describing the present or downright politically objectionable.

In chapter 3, I'll offer a broad context for this paradox by accounting for why "culture" became such an important keyword in this specific period. But for now, we must simply note that one of the central gambits of the cultural turn, especially for anthropologists, was to identify and critique what they saw as an outmoded, inadequate, and stubbornly persistent usage of "culture." For many critics of culture emerging from this context, including not only Clifford but also Renato Rosaldo, Arjun Appadurai, and Lila Abu-Lughod, to name just a few, the concept is plainly still too connotative of an older way of thinking. It sneaks in subtle or not-so-subtle assumptions about homogeneity, purity, boundedness, and authenticity that are ultimately connected to an imperialist will to power over the colonial subject, the equally reified entity designated the "native." Moreover, this flies in the face of all other evidence that shows that culture is not rigid and reducible to static "patterns" but mobile, plastic, and promiscuous. The interesting stuff is not what fits but what doesn't; what exists on the borders and complicates assumed values, hierarchies, and categories, including those of self and other.

Of course, as a number of commentators on the doing-away-with-culture phenomenon have already observed, the older anthropological usages of culture were hardly as rigid, as invested in boundaries and stability, as many of their detractors made them out to be.[2] Indeed, immersion in the history of the discipline has often proven quite the opposite, and a diverse group of anthropologists (but especially those in the Boasian tradition) have been recuperated precisely on the grounds that not only are they sophisticated thinkers about culture, but they anticipate this or that aspect of the cultural turn.[3] Nevertheless, as Clifford's futuristic thought experiment indicates, there is a strong progressivist tendency to rewrite the discipline as one of a benighted past unfolding into an increasingly enlightened present. Thus Rosaldo for one contextualizes his refutation of the "classic norms" of his discipline, including the culture concept and traditional ethnographic practice, with an admitted "caricature" of disciplinary history, beginning with the figure of an imperialist "Lone Ethnographer." This figure of the "heroic period" and the "birth of ethnography" is subsequently supplanted in the equally composite moment of "classic ethnography" (1921–71).[4]

Rosaldo's demarcation of this second period gets us closer to a plausible critical target of the cultural turn. It is the moment of Ruth Benedict's widely influential conception of distinctive cultural "patterns" modeled along the lines of personality types, the wide influence of British structural functionalism, Parsonian conceptions of social determination, and structuralism proper. In other words, what is really being critiqued in the caricature of older conceptions of culture is not so much "culture" but structuralist, culture-and-personality, and social-determinist deployments of the concept, all of which could fairly be seen, from the perspective of the cultural turn, as overemphasizing homogeneity, coherence, stability, and so forth. Which is to say, this moment also generally deemphasized individual agency, an issue of increasing interest to scholars of the post-1968 generation. This is the larger context for reading one of Arjun Appadurai's central complaints against culture: "The noun *culture* appears to privilege the sort of sharing, agreeing, and bounding that fly in the face of the facts of unequal knowledge and the differential prestige of lifestyles, and to discourage attention to the worldviews and agency of those who are marginalized or dominated."[5]

The result of this culturalist critique of culture has been a twofold fastidiousness. First, it is almost obligatory in the literature of anthropology to state concern and skepticism about culture as a guiding concept on the predictable grounds of its reifying tendencies, followed by some palliative methodological proposals, such as refining one's usage of "culture" in some specific way, or abstaining from nominatives and using only the adjectival form "cultural."[6] But such gestures also imply, and are part and parcel of, a general phobia about reification, resulting in a deep hermeneutic suspicion of generalizations of any kind.[7] Lila Abu-Lughod, in her widely cited essay "Writing against Culture," states, "If 'culture,' shadowed by coherence, timelessness, and discreteness, is the prime anthropological tool for making "other," and difference, as feminists and halfies [people of mixed cultural identity] reveal, tends to be a relationship of power, then perhaps anthropologists should consider strategies for writing against culture."[8] One of her central strategies for writing against culture, the creation of "ethnographies of the particular," takes explicit aim at the sin of generalization and its attendant associations of abstraction and objectivity.[9]

In the midst of this panic over reification, it seems more than a little scandalous to ask, Is it always such a bad thing? There is a compelling reason why anthropologists in particular might be pressed on this point, for, as many have lately noted, sometimes with ill-concealed dismay, there are probably no people left on earth who do not assume that they have something called a "culture." While many such people can speak with a great deal of sophistication about that fact, such indigenous views of culture are certainly not fastidiously avoidant of reifications. Christoph Brumann puts the case as follows: "Whether anthropologists like it or not, it appears that people—and not only those with power—*want* culture, and they often want it precisely in the bounded, reified, essentialized, and timeless fashion that most of us now reject. Moreover, just like other concepts such as 'tribe,' culture has become a political and judicial reality."[10]

Such "reflexivization" has long been considered a hallmark of what it means to be a subject in modernity: being able to conceive of oneself as embedded within historical time and space.[11] To be Hopi or Fijian is no longer a matter of unselfconsciously going about one's (premodern) life but an active form of identity construction and maintenance. And this is also, of course, a clear example of culture's reification. Each of these specific cultures is now a thing out there in the world, which means that each is also susceptible to the commodification, theft, and investment of aura that characterize all of our modern identities. Hopi culture is now fully available to the uses and abuses of tourism, New Age nonsense, the art market, school, and copyright law.[12] All of which explains the tristesse over this reification, which (as Claude Lévi-Strauss once helped us see) is in no small part sorrow for our own fallen selves.[13] But we may as well be honest that this desire for a prereflexivized world holds a tang of romantic othering and acknowledge that there are both ethical and practical difficulties in wishing to deny someone this self-conscious sense of cultural identity, even with all its attendant theoretical problems.

All of which brings us to what we might call the romantic heart of the anthropological cultural turn. In the context not only of obvious and objectionable forms of cultural reification (as, say, in the South African usage of the idea of cultural difference to justify racial apartheid) but also of the nascent globalization that Clifford so clearly recognized, all that complexity and particularity, all those liminal cases and things that failed to fit the categories serve another function: to describe an ineffable culture that might be seen to avoid reification and thus somehow to slip out of the bonds of market logic.[14] In a moment of the complete commodification of culture, perhaps culture could be so reconstituted to still mark a space of externality—of possibility. Of course, this space of externality is almost by definition indefinable—which brings me to complaint number 2.

2. THERE IS NO SUCH THING AS CULTURE

While the critiques of culture that emerged from within the cultural turn worried over the problem of the term's reification, its danger-ous solidity, another critique of culture of long standing has gone in precisely the opposite direction. No less a figure in anthropology than the famed British structuralist Mary Douglas once put the matter as follows: "Never was such a fluffy notion at large in a self-styled scientific discipline, not since singing angels blew the planets across the medieval sky or ether filled in the gaps of Newton's universe."[15] For critics of culture such as Douglas, the problem is not culture's excessive solidity of meaning but precisely the opposite: if it is not an entirely meaningless abstraction, then it is certainly a "hyper-referential" concept in strong need of some reining in.[16]

According to Adam Kuper, "culture" simply connotes too much, is too messy, and needs to be broken up into its various components— "knowledge, or belief, or art, or technology, or tradition, or even . . . ideology"—in order to be properly analyzed.[17] This list is itself telling: Kuper relegates to "culture" items that in a Marxist tradition might be called "superstructural." But this also implies a base. Kuper writes, "Political and economic forces, social institutions, and biological pro-cesses cannot be wished away, or assimilated to systems of knowledge and belief. And that, I will suggest, is the ultimate stumbling block in the way of cultural theory, certainly given its current pretensions."[18] In other words, there are things that are simply, irreducibly, not cultural. Moreover, there are things that are not explainable *culturally*. The dif-ficulties really start for Kuper when "culture shifts from something to be described, interpreted, even perhaps explained, and is treated instead as a source of explanation in itself."[19]

I will get to a discussion of Kuper's specific criticisms, but first it is important to note that he is hardly alone in suggesting that there are other fundamental areas that cannot be "wished away, or assimilated to systems of knowledge and belief." Indeed, a very prominent strain of complaint against culture is that it fails to account for the "real" processes of human existence: the political, the economic, the social, or the biological.

For the prominent evolutionary psychologists John Tooby and Leda Cosmides, "culture" has too long been the retreat of social scientists, whom they caricature as adhering to a rigid set of scientifically insupportable ideas about the human mind and an equally rigid superstructural model of culture in order to avoid acknowledgment of the basic biological foundations of human existence.[20] In a thought experiment, they offer an interesting snapshot of how human behavior might be characterized, and of how the idea of culture might be put in its place:

> Imagine that extraterrestrials replaced each human being on earth with a state-of-the-art compact disk juke box that has thousands of songs in its repertoire. Each juke box is identical. Moreover, each is equipped with a clock, an automated navigational device that measures its latitude and longitude, and a circuit that selects what song it will play on the basis of its location, the time, and the date. What our extraterrestrials would observe would be the same kind of pattern of within-group similarities and between-group differences observable among humans: In Rio, every juke box would be playing the same song, which would be different from the song that every juke box was playing in Beijing, and so on, around the world.[21]

According to Tooby and Cosmides, each of these juke boxes would appear to behave like a "cultured" being in the following senses: because its original playlist of songs was large and diverse, its actual program of played songs would seem "complexly patterned"; because its programming was directed by a clock, its behavior would change over time; and because its navigational sensors required it to change its repertoire with any change in location, it would appear to "adapt" to new surroundings. But all these behaviors are products of the relationship between the environment and a "highly organized architecture that is richly endowed with contentful mechanisms."[22] Tooby and Cosmides suggest that if this be considered culture at all, then it should be denominated as "evoked" culture, as distinct from what they consider the far more restricted field of "epidemiological" culture: behavior learned, or transmitted like the flu, from one person to another. Indeed, conspicuously absent from their thought experiment is any such consideration of inter–juke box learning or interaction: though all juke boxes may share a common "architecture," they are strict individualists.[23]

Ultimately, of course, what interests the evolutionary psychologists is not the culture but the "architecture." But what, exactly is this, and where does it reside? Clearly, it is a product of evolutionary processes, and therefore it ultimately returns us to both our genetic makeup and the often rather speculative history of our species, with special attention to Pleistocene hunter-gatherers.[24] The brain is also frequently evoked, as is the mind, as the repository of complex, "contentful" "modules" of human ability and behavior. This, we may say, is evolutionary psychology's base to the superstructural airiness of culture. But as Barbara Herrnstein Smith points out in her critique of evolutionary psychology, it's not as if this base ever goes entirely to ground. The brain here is not exactly the physical brain of the neuroscientists, while "the mind," as ever, is less a resolution to the problem of the relationship between behavior and biology than a statement of it. Rather, according to Smith, what the abstraction of "the mind" allows evolutionary psychologists to do is simply to posit another version of a familiar dualist model inherited both from the Chomskian linguistics to which they are indebted and from the longer tradition of rationalism. In another classic version of the traditional dualisms, culture (or human behavior) is the appearance to the reality of complex, information-rich modules.[25]

Thus is one apparent abstraction (culture) banished, via the free deployment of another (the mind). This situation is entirely of a piece with other such attempts to wave away the apparent abstractions of culture by returning to the spurious solidity of something else. As Richard Handler notes in his refusal of this gesture by the editors of the volume *Beyond the Cultural Turn*, their rejection of culture for the "social" only seems to imply a comforting concreteness, when it is no less imprecise than "culture" as a term. Moreover, taken as a pair in this way, culture and the social simply become yet another dualism of reality and appearance, truth and illusion—or, as Handler interestingly notes, body and mind.[26]

But isn't there some merit to the charge that culture has become too unwieldy—"hyper-referential"? I have written elsewhere about the tendency—again, typical of the moment of the cultural turn—to equate culture with totality, and about the not-uncommon reaction to this that regards the category of culture as too capacious.[27] So I will grant that there are all sorts of good reasons for wanting to maintain a categorical separation between culture and other arenas, which one might wish to designate the social, biological, economic, or what have you. But as with any such implicit division, certain obvious questions arise, especially about how these various parts are then related to one another. For example, how is politics related to ideology? (Kuper asserts that politics cannot be "assimilated to systems of knowledge and belief," whereas others—Karl Marx, for one—consider politics part of the superstructure.) Do these arenas that cannot be "wished away" then have some kind of determinative impact on the content of the "cultural" sphere, or vice versa, or is culture something best understood as rigidly separate? There are a number of possible ways to address this issue, including a theory of mediation, in which other features of the human condition—even such presumably material items as "political and economic forces, social institutions, and biological processes"—are understood through and within a cultural matrix. In other words, saying that "everything is mediated by culture" is not the same thing as saying "everything *is* culture"; totalization (the process of making connections) is not the same as totality.[28]

Of course, Kuper's other complaint, that it is a grave error to consider culture "a source of explanation in itself," makes it clear that he holds no interest in any theory of cultural mediation. Instead, he reduces such an idea to a category error, in which his limited set of cultural objects (belief, ideology, etc.) are not seen properly as the objects of explanation but erroneously as the sources or conduits of it. But we might as well concede that something else is at work in these efforts to put culture in its place. Ultimately, they reflect a desire to take all the conflict out of culture, for if it is mere appearance, superstructure, a small set of describable phenomena, then it is certainly not a difficult site of contestation over meaning itself.

3. CULTURE IS NOTHING MORE THAN A SNEAKY WAY OF TALKING ABOUT RACE

As Kuper forthrightly acknowledges, there are long-standing national elements to the critique of culture. A native South African and a British-trained social anthropologist, Kuper is doubly poised to dismiss culture, which he describes as a largely American preoccupation. Kuper was impressed early and forcibly by culture's use as a central feature of national ideology in South Africa, where the preservation of distinctive native cultures was offered as a rationale for apartheid. Moreover, like Mary Douglas, he inherited from A. R. Radcliffe-Brown—an important founder of British anthropology who also spent formative time in South Africa—an emphasis on social structure as the central object of analysis, and a corresponding dismissal of culture as a mere "abstraction."[29]

Reference to South African apartheid should remind us that this critique of culture, like so many others, carries with it a powerful moral charge. Implicitly or explicitly, culture's main function as a (mere) rhetorical construct signals not only its ethereal nothingness but its availability to more sinister uses: "culture" is used to say things that might be more precisely, but less politely, expressed by other obsolete or objectionable concepts such as race, nation, class, or even blood. Thus, just as the notorious example of South African apartheid is frequently invoked in arguments against the term, it is also often pointed out that "culture" serves to bolster class and ethnic distinctions by designating the specific heritage and arts practices of elites.[30] Without such disturbing connotations, it is suggested, culture as a concept would be useless; with these connotations, it is best left unsaid.

Though many critics of "culture" have suggested its affinity to such objectionable or outmoded terms as "race," literary scholar Walter Benn Michaels has offered perhaps the most extended discussion of this connection. In *Our America* (1995), Michaels argues that the general multiculturalist American discourse of identity is simply a tricky way of talking about racial identity without making reference to race, or to a Social Darwinist's conception of "blood," which is race's ultimate reference.[31] A tenacious debunker of liberal pieties, Michaels is in general concerned to critique a sometimes unthinking relationship to cultural discourse that a more obviously conservative writer might be tempted to call political correctness. Following a familiar argumentative structure in which he shows how his opponents are engaging in the very thing they would wish to repudiate, Michaels argues that those who would see culture as a more malleable way to think about identity are in fact recapitulating an older racism that they would doubtless find abhorrent. In a simple sense, then, what Michaels really seems to advocate is a radical and thoroughgoing repudiation of biological determinism. If this racist kind of thinking about human difference is unacceptable, he concludes, then cultural thinking, its cognate, should be too.

We could take up any number of issues here, perhaps the most obvious being the question of Michaels's goals in launching this line of critique. Not without reason, he has been read as supporting the kind of juridical race-blindness advocated by many American conservatives.[32] But as his recent book *The Shape of the Signifier* (2004) clarifies, his desire to do away with both race and culture is part of a more concerted critique of identity itself. Returning to his early "Against Theory" essays, Michaels grounds his critique of subjectivity in a problem of literary interpretation: either you believe that meaning is there to be found in the text, or you believe that it is generated in the mind of the individual reader. In this fundamental division—which he locates as emerging with the development of literary theory in the 1960s—Michaels comes down squarely on the side that would say that meaning resides in the text. Indeed, he asserts that it is the job of interpretation to recover authorial intent. This problem of authorial intent is one of the most vexing features of Michaels's work in that he never really addresses what it might entail: Does the author's intention stay the same over the course of the creation of a work? Can there be unconscious intent? Could the author's intention be the product of forces outside the author's direct control? Rather than addressing these issues, which might even lead him back to some conception of a socially embedded meaning within a text, Michaels concentrates on what he sees as the disturbing political and theoretical consequences of the opposing view of meaning as residing in the subjective reading experience. Central among these consequences, he argues, is an overinvestment in identity, of which race and culture are simply versions.[33]

Michaels's central concern about identity, repetitively offered throughout both of his last two books, boils down to the following: the descriptive proposition "We do/believe this because we have this cultural identity" soon becomes the prescriptive maxim "Because we have this cultural identity, we do/believe this." In a sense, then, Michaels's complaint against culture is *both* that it is an insubstantial nothing *and* that as a marker of identity it is too concrete. On the one hand, "culture" is a rhetorical sleight, a mere code word for "race," whose own ultimate referent and political significance in turn is a kind of biological determinism. On the other hand, insofar as "culture" connotes identity, which he worries is far too determinative of people's behavior and belief, culture is a reification. Ultimately, Michaels may well be a kind of existentialist, whose ideal is a space of radical freedom from externally imposed identity. If so, it is a position that unites him in some interesting ways with the likes of (Sartre-influenced) French philosopher Alain Badiou, who has explicitly rejected as vacuous any ethics based on a conception of cultural difference.[34]

But let us return to Michaels's case for the connection between race and culture. In *Our America,* one of his central examples for the proposition that "culture" is no more than a code word for "race" is that of Lothrop Stoddard, author of *The Rising Tide of Color against White World-Supremacy* (1920). According to Michaels, Stoddard abandoned his earlier arguments for white racial superiority when taking up the question of European immigration. In Stoddard's view, America's distinctiveness, not the relative inferiority of others, was the only necessary fact and rationale for defending it against the encroachments of foreigners. Stoddard's arguments confirm for Michaels that cultural pluralism conforms not only to the needs of nationalist bigotry but to racism. Indeed, "It is precisely this pluralism that transforms the substitution of culture for race into the preservation of race. For pluralism's programmatic hostility to universalism—its hostility to the idea that cultural practices be justified by appeals to what seems universally good or true—requires that such practices be justified instead by appeals to what seems locally good or true, which is to say, it invokes the identity of the group as the grounds for the justification of the group's practices."[35] But again, this is not ultimately a statement about culture (or race) so much as it is about identity. A more penetrating look at the xenophobic uses of cultural discourse—now taken from a modern example with clear similarities to that of Stoddard—may shed light on how this objectionable field of culture is currently operating.

Since World War II, there has been a more or less official ban on racist rhetoric in most of western Europe. Yet there are those who publicly espouse prejudicial sentiments, especially against immigrants. And, as a number of observers have pointed out, they have couched their prejudices in terms of "culture." A notorious example of such cultural rhetoric was Margaret Thatcher's 1978 comment: "People are really rather afraid that this country might be swamped by people of a different culture. And, you know, the British character has done so much for democracy, for law, and done so much throughout the world, that if there is a fear that it might be swamped, people are going to react and be hostile to those coming in."[36] Thatcher's words would soon be identified as part of a concerted New Right effort to define an exclusive, but explicitly nonracist, British identity.[37] They also contain many of the elements of European xenophobia with which we have become familiar: the assertion of a uniquely British (and implicitly superior) culture being overwhelmed by alien and incompatible cultures, conjoined with the implicit or explicit assumption that it is reasonable to wish to defend that culture from the onslaught.

Certainly, there are parallels between this rhetoric and traditional racism, not the least being the invocation of a sense of biological menace implicit in the reiterated idea of being "swamped" and the overweening and aggressive expressions of pride in the superiority of the dominant group. But as Verena Stolcke has pointed out, there are also important differences between this rhetoric, however objectionable, and that of traditional racism. In her view, modern racism represents a justification of the inferiority of social underlings so that patent inequities of society and of opportunity are transposed back upon the racial others, as products of their own well-understood, inherently inferior, attributes. With the rhetoric of xenophobia, however, the targets are aliens: outsiders to the nation-state. There is no assumption of either knowledge or inferiority of the other; rather, what is emphasized is incommensurability between "us" and the ineffable alien, and an inherent and wholly justifiable human inclination toward ethnocentrism and xenophobia. Thus modern racism and what Stolcke calls "cultural fundamentalism" are useful to their adherents because they seem to offer satisfying resolutions to two very different ideological problems. While modern racism conceptually resolves the apparent contradiction in the ideology of liberal democracy between equal opportunity and meritocracy, cultural fundamentalism works within the interstices of another great liberal contradiction: the UN-era civic religion of universal humanity rubbing up against the obvious facts of human difference and conflict.[38]

At least in the context of right-wing anti-immigrant sentiment in Europe, then, the rhetoric of culture is in no simple sense a replacement for racist rhetoric. Nor does it appear that race is an adequate interpretive frame for unraveling the complexities of, say, American xenophobia after September 11.[39] As for Michaels's other conclusion, that cultural identity has become the determinant of thought or behavior, this case proves a bit more contradictory. Indeed, it seems that precisely the problem of immigration, and of many measures directed toward ameliorating its effects, is that there is a great deal of public uncertainty about the relationship between culture, belief, and behavior. Will banning hijabs in public schools make Muslim girls more French? Will insisting that the U.S. national anthem be sung in English foster a more culturally coherent form of Americanness? This problem of culture and belief will be addressed more extensively in chapter 5.

4. CULTURE IS POLITICALLY CONSERVATIVE

As Fredric Jameson showed, Michaels's work has long been characterized as operating via a logic of homology. In Michaels's recent book, these homologous juxtapositions are sometimes arrayed in baffling logical forms (e.g., "If you think that differences in belief cannot be described as differences in identity, you must also think that texts mean what their authors intend" or "If you hold, say, Judith Butler's views on resignification, you will also be required to hold, say, George W. Bush's views on terrorism") that tend to suggest some greater axiomatic reach, some address to a larger cultural logic.[40] In a subsequent essay, Michaels denominates this cultural logic as neoliberalism, the political economic order whose central ideological characteristic is its postideological, posthistorical transcendence of all opposing systems; its central slogan-to-end-all-slogans, coined by Margaret Thatcher and her allies, is TINA, "There is no alternative."[41] Michaels's trenchant critique of culture is thus, in essence, that it participates in this postideological TINA thinking, in which an obsession with identity (for that's what culture is) masks the central—that is, economic and political—divisions and antagonisms within our society: "Culture . . . has become the primary technology for disarticulating difference from disagreement" and for "disarticulating difference from inequality."[42] This is powerful stuff, made all the more so because Michaels connects it to a broad historical and theoretical frame. This is also, according to Michaels, the logic of postmodernism and a wide variety of novels and literary theories (because they privilege subjectivity and therefore identity), and a whole host of postideological positions and theories, from the war on terror to the "biopolitics" of Michael Hardt and Antonio Negri's *Empire*.

As my discussion of the new conservative uses of "culture" should illustrate, it is not at all clear to me that culture currently functions as a way to mask conflict. Indeed, Terry Eagleton, who also hinges his critique of culture on an antipathy to identity politics, points out that "in Bosnia or Belfast, culture is not just what you put on the cassette player; it is what you kill for."[43] But Michaels's criticism is directed, not at the combatants in the world's hot spots, or even at garden-variety xenophobes and culture warriors, but at a (neo-)liberal academic reader. As such, it partakes of another long-standing strain of complaint about culture, namely that despite whatever alignments it currently suggests (and whoever espouses it or its cognates), culture is conservative at its core. Quoting Eagleton again (here working against his other point): "Culture is . . . an antidote to politics, tempering that fanatical tunnel vision in its appeal to equipoise, to keeping the mind serenely untainted by whatever is tendentious, unbalanced, sectarian."[44] This criticism is particularly strong in the Anglo-American literary tradition, where some of culture's most notable exponents have included conservative figures like Edmund Burke, Samuel Taylor Coleridge, and T. S. Eliot, and where the hidden or not-so hidden context of the discourse of culture has been reaction to the horrors of the French Revolution and whatever "anarchy" the masses might subsequently throw up.

In his landmark *Culture and Society* (1958), Raymond Williams tried to recuperate this conservative tradition for the progressive ends of a revivified working-class culture. But at least by some lights, this project was a failure. According to David Lloyd and Paul Thomas, Williams's work traces a history of culture that is largely synonymous with the Arnoldian project of the education of "best selves," which is seen as a necessary precondition for universal political enfranchisement—a necessary guard, in other words, against the disruptions of the status quo caused by real working-class politics. Lloyd and Thomas show that there is another, explicitly political working-class tradition that rejects the idea of cultural/educational prerequisites to political empowerment. For them, Williams doesn't so much recuperate a tradition for progressive ends as simply replicate the conservative logic of the politically dominant position.[45]

This would be a powerful critique if Arnold were indeed the central figure of *Culture and Society*. Certainly, Arnold represents a punctuation mark in Williams's book, as befits a central codifier of culture in the British tradition. But rather than describing Arnold's particular achievement as the last word on culture (before moving on to a host of other figures), Williams portrays Arnold's culture as precisely the reification of a line of cultural theory begun by Arnold's conservative predecessors, including Burke, Coleridge, and Cardinal Newman.[46] In other words, Arnold's is not the culture that Williams is interested in recuperating. Nor is it exactly that for Williams there are other, or parallel, traditions to be excavated—say, a tradition emanating from his more radical cast of figures including William Cobbett, Robert Owen, Thomas Carlyle, and William Morris, who took as their lesson from the French Revolution not a fear of the mob but the possibility of actively making history. Rather, *all* of these figures, the conservatives and the radicals together, are responding in their different veins to another desire: to unite the pieces of human existence shattered by the experience of modernity itself. Culture for Williams, then, is a discursive space marking out a desire for wholeness: not the reified spatial wholeness that makes the anthropologists so nervous but a moving, processual, creation and coming into being that entails the unity not only of such putatively separate spheres as the arts, education, politics, and economics but also of the individual and society.

This was a vision that would lead Williams inevitably to Marxism, but certainly not to what he called the "rationalist" part of that tradition that sectioned off culture, or some of its perceived components such as art or belief, into a separate or "superstructural" sphere. This idea, Williams wrote, "has come to overlay and stifle Marxism, with some warrant in its most obvious errors, but without having to face the real challenge which was implicit, and so nearly clarified in the original Marxist intervention."[47] Rather, what attracted Williams to Marxism was its refusal of such separations in its trenchant identification and critique of reification and alienation and in its "recovery of the wholeness of history." We may think here, for example, of Marx's famous countervision to the modern division of labor, in which one might "hunt in the morning, fish in the afternoon, rear cattle in the evening, criticize after dinner."[48] As for the Marxist conception of history, Williams wrote: "The original notion of 'man making his own history' was given a new radical content by this emphasis on 'man making himself' through producing his own means of life. For all its difficulties in detailed demonstration this was the most important intellectual advance in all modern social thought. It offered the possibility of overcoming the dichotomy between 'society' and 'nature,' and of discovering new constitutive relationships between 'society' and 'economy.' As a specification of the basic element of the social process of culture it was a recovery of the wholeness of history."[49]

All of which is, of course, to say that culture is—or at least can be—a fundamentally dialectical proposition. William Ray locates within the complexity of culture, which he reads back into eighteenth- and nineteenth-century European thought, a deeply dialectical "logic": "If [culture] accommodates so many competing accounts, it is because it frames truth, law, and identity not as stable structures or unvarying doctrines, but as the constantly changing products of *a dialectic between individual initiatives of understanding and the rules and traditions which undergird them—and are continually being revised by them.*"[50] Though Ray's analysis limits the logic of culture to one dialectical operation between the individual and society (I will want to explore others as well), it nevertheless serves as an important rejoinder to static conceptions such as Michaels's of culture *as* (a subset of) identity.

Indeed, with this general insight about culture as what Ray calls a "strategy" for understanding the dialectical relationships of certain key propositions, we can revisit the dismissals of culture by the evolutionary psychologists, as well as the complaints against culture leveled by the anthropologists of the cultural turn. Cultural evolutionists Peter J. Richerson and Robert Boyd offer satisfying refutations to the view that behavior is all in our genes by grappling with the truly complex, dialectical interactions of environment, genetic makeup, and learned behavior. They write, for example, "Selection shapes individual learning mechanisms so that interaction with the environment produces adaptive behavior."[51] As for the anthropologists of the cultural turn, in their various concerns about the reifications of older and other conceptions of culture, we may now see them as attempting to unstick a reified conception of culture in favor of a dialectical understanding, which would, say, place the local practices of a given group of people into play with considerations of larger forces and processes (call them patterns, if you like, or structures). Their mistake has been to see the way out of reification in an ever-more scrupulous attention to particularity, when instead they might consider the significance of the dialectical operation that lay within their original critique of the concept.

Finally, it is only by attending to these issues of dialectics—which is to say, these issues of culture's real complexity—that we can properly read powerful critiques such as Herbert Marcuse's "The Affirmative Character of Culture." Marcuse describes "affirmative culture," a specific product of the bourgeois era, as simultaneously upholding the status quo and offering a powerful critique of its rationalizations of human life. "Its decisive characteristic is the assertion of a universally obligatory, eternally better and more valuable world that must be unconditionally affirmed: a world essentially different from the factual world of the daily struggle for existence, yet realizable by every individual for himself 'from within,' without any transformation of the state of fact."[52] The central critical nugget of this culture, its utopian critique of the bourgeois culture that created it, thus soon succumbs to reification not only in celebrated cultural artifacts but in the work of the individual to become cultured: "Culture means not so much a better world as a nobler one: a world to be brought about not through the overthrow of the material order of life but through events in the individual's soul."[53] Marcuse's solution to this problem is the "abolition of this culture," which can come about only through a complete transformation of the "material order of life." But in its place must come culture. "The reproduction of life will still involve culture: the molding of unfulfilled longings and the purification of unfulfilled instincts."[54]

5. CULTURE IS SUBSTITUTE RELIGION

Now that "wholeness" (and utopia) are on the table, we must turn to one final critique of culture, which holds that ultimately it is nothing more than a kind of secular religion. In general, this critique is a logical corollary to the idea that culture is inherently conservative, for it simply extends to culture the suspicion that religion is nothing more than an agent of stupefaction for the masses.

This argument has a number of variants. One strain of it, a close cousin of the guilt-by-association logic of the assertion that culture is inherently conservative, cites figures such as T. S. Eliot (again), for whom religion and culture were indeed closely linked. For Eliot, religion was in effect as close as the benighted masses could get to culture, which entailed not only a minute observance of the rituals of daily life of a certain place (say, England) but a priestly understanding of them as well.[55] Working in a vein similar to Eliot's but arriving at the precise opposite point, Slavoj Žižek suggests that culture's current meaning boils down to religion (or rather, ritual) shorn of belief—as in the phrase "I don't really believe in it, it's just part of my culture."[56] From the perspective of at least one important theological tradition, where the burning issue is the place of the faithful in relation to the surrounding "culture," both of these propositions seem a little startling.[57]

Another variant of this critique grounds itself in historical arguments such as Marcuse's that culture has served as a central site of the critique of modernity. If modernity, as the Weberian story goes, is characterized by its increasing disenchantment, then surely culture's critique of modernity is at heart religious. Culture, then, entails some sort of return to a prelapsarian fantasy world, preceding all the divisions and reifications that bedevil modernity, not the least being that between religion and daily life. Geoffrey H. Hartman, who takes this view, suggests that we are then haunted by this fantasy: "'Culture' at present—I mean the ring and function of the word, its emotional and conceptual resonance—even when it is abusively applied, keeps hope in embodiment alive. Consciousness, as ghostly as ever, cannot renounce that hope in a living and fulfilling milieu."[58] Culture, a spectral presence, is something that still calls to us out of our premodern past. But perhaps there is a different way to look at things, which addresses our desire, not for a more embodied being associated with the past, but for futurity.

There is a somewhat strained moment in *The Predicament of Culture* when Clifford juxtaposes the innovative ethnographic film *Trobriand Cricket* with Picasso's famous painting *Les Demoiselles d'Avignon*. Clifford points to a scene in the film in which a Trobriand Islander is shown simultaneously umpiring the game of cricket, incanting spells, and eating betel nuts out of a blue plastic Adidas bag. Clifford suggests that an attention to such surprising juxtapositions, such "ethnographic surrealism[,] can help us see the blue plastic Adidas bag as part of the same kind of inventive cultural process as the African-looking masks that in 1907 suddenly appeared attached to the pink bodies of the *Demoiselles d'Avignon.*"[59]

To a contemporary reader used to anecdotes about globalization's promiscuous trafficking in goods and peoples, Clifford's effusion over the exotically located plastic bag (which Clifford declares to be "beautiful") naively overestimates the scene's significance. In retrospect, this enthusiasm for mixture and indeterminacy now seems characteristic of the cultural turn, which developed not only a taste for "pure products gone crazy" (to paraphrase Clifford, paraphrasing William Carlos Williams) but an excessive interpretive emphasis on the ineffable effects of an endlessly mutable and creative and certainly borderless "culture." But what we might call this aesthetic of the cultural turn also had a political dimension. The strain in Clifford's anecdote, the hyperbolic claim that the casual appropriation of a plastic bag is somehow comparable to the creative gesture of painting the work that inaugurated cubism, reveals the wish that some ineffable something—something profound, revolutionary—will emerge from the interstices of this kind of cultural contact. That is, something will emerge that escapes reification and market logic and reorganizes our conception of social space in the moment of globalization.

When Hartman offers us his Romantic take on spectral culture, he is of course alluding to Derrida's more famous argument that we (the subjects of neoliberalism) are haunted by Marx.[60] This chapter has offered nothing but evidence for such an idea. For, if we consider the complaints against culture, they uncannily replicate those that have long been leveled against Marxism. Both culture and Marxism have been critiqued on the grounds of structural rigidity and insufficient suppleness with regard to the particularities of location, position, agency. Both have been implicated in critiques of "totality." Both have been accused of being romantic; false politics; false religion; false utopianism. So what, indeed, are we trying to dispel when we get rid of culture? Perhaps the last spectral whiff of another way. If culture shares these currents with Marxism, it is because it remains one of our best, most complex, discursive fields for conceptualizing possibility in the context of the closure of neoliberalism.

I would not say that we are haunted by culture; rather, we are haunted by the idea of a futurity—articulated through an idea of culture—that in our current political and philosophical moment seems unavailable to us. Or rather, we are haunted by certain cultures, whose meanings seem inaccessible to us now precisely because of the closures of historical possibility. This, I believe, is the case with the concept of "mass culture," the subject of the next chapter, whose political power can be understood only when it is restored to its specific critical context within modernism and the years before World War II.

CHAPTER 2

Haunted by Mass Culture

To say that culture is a concept that mediates between parts and wholes is all well and good. But it's important as well to recognize the historical specificity of what those parts and wholes are. Here, I take up one particular well-known usage of the idea of culture, "mass culture"—a historically specific phenomenon, dependent upon a complex, modern arrangement of social life—to demonstrate the workings of culture as a dialectical concept within a particular historical situation. The ultimate goal will be to shed some light on the meaning of "mass culture" and some of the terms it is often compared to or elided with, especially "popular culture" and "mass media."

Like "culture," "mass culture" is a complex term of art in the context of a relatively capacious set of debates about the relationship between the activities of daily life and politics. In particular, "mass culture" appears alongside questions of how political and positional subjectivities are created and suppressed; the relationship between propaganda and the public and private spheres; and how to articulate the connections between different kinds of cultural audiences, forms, and styles: elite, youth, minority, subcultural, countercultural, and so forth. Finally, like "culture" as a whole, the debates that "mass culture" signals have come to seem both passé and wearying, artifactual of other intellectual moments. Which is to say that "mass culture," like culture as a whole, has experienced its own reification. It has become especially ossified into the framework of two easily caricatured, and ultimately convergent, debates: the first, about *art* versus mass culture; the second about *popular culture* versus mass culture. Both of these debates have their origins around World War II and its immediate aftermath, and both were revived in different ways during the cultural turn.

In the United States the idea of art versus mass culture is generally traceable back to the *Partisan Review* writers Clement Greenberg and Dwight Macdonald. Greenberg, primarily an art critic, would establish one of the most influential theoretical statements about modernist art in the United States. This was just in time to have maximal influence in the postwar period, when global hegemony had shifted to the United States and, correspondingly, the center of gravity of the art world had shifted from Paris to New York. Starting with his famous essay "Avant-Garde and Kitsch" (1939), Greenberg posited a definition of avant-garde art as art that was formally self-referential: paintings (like those of the abstract expressionists that Greenberg would champion) about painting. Everything else—any art that was tied in any way to extratextual ideas or narratives—was relegated to the dustbin of "kitsch."

As many commentators have noted, this move also positioned Greenberg as the central art critic of the cold war period, in that his primary goal behind this distinction was to separate art from propaganda. Though the ostensible object of this separation was the form of realist art officially supported by the Soviet government, it also implicitly or explicitly indicted a great deal of American art created out of a prewar context much more sympathetic to leftist and even liberal and populist agendas, including the art favored by the Popular Front's American Artists' Congress and the WPA art projects. Macdonald, in turn, would help cement the connection between non-art and propaganda through a telling and influential neologism, "masscult," which made the idea of a culture of or for the masses sound scary and even a bit Russian (as in "Proletkult").[1] Much of American art history, henceforth, would parallel American literary history. The cold war–era dedication to aesthetic formalism (in concert with the high moment of new critical literary formalism) would increasingly find challenges in new, more politicized and historicized approaches. By the time of the publication of Serge Guilbaut's *How New York Stole the Idea of Modern Art* (1983), it would become de rigueur to challenge Greenberg's highly rarified definition of art on a number of grounds: its antipolitical subtext, its historically limited view of the avant-garde's engagement with popular forms, and, perhaps ultimately less interesting, its apparent elitism.[2]

One unfortunate result of this challenge to the Greenbergian ortho-doxy was the establishment of a certain caricature of modernism. For proponents of postmodernism especially, Greenberg's formalist defini-tion of art was often taken as the definition of modernism as a whole, and as a result it became a postmodernist truism that modernist art was difficult, elitist, and inherently opposed to mass culture. It seems clearer now that modernism in its moment was far more diverse and far more complex in its relationship to mass-circulated forms than post-modernist ideologues gave it credit for. Indeed, as Fredric Jameson has argued, what the postmodernists were responding to in their critiques of Greenberg and company was not modernism in its historical actuality but an *ideology* of modernism, proposed retrospectively, in the moment of its institutionalization.[3] At any rate, it hardly seems necessary any longer to argue that either modernist art or art as a whole ever held itself in rigid opposition, or even antipathy, to mass culture.

The second debate surrounding mass culture also in some ways traces its intellectual antecedents back to this rigid opposition between art and mass culture. Though explicitly associated with the emergent field of cul-tural studies, the opposition between mass culture and popular culture is often seen as having its roots in the work of members of the exiled Frankfurt School. These figures—especially Theodor Adorno and Max Horkheimer—are often portrayed as upholding the same mass culture/art distinction as Greenberg and Macdonald. In this fairly common view, Adorno and Horkheimer are leftist mandarins, bemoaning the loss of European culture in the face of the onslaught of the dreck produced by the American "culture industry." While it is true that the *Partisan Review* writers did at times claim common cause with Adorno and company, the comparison is only superficial. Adorno and Horkheimer always saw art's autonomy as imperfect, paid for at the cost of other political and social constraints. (Put in the terms of their powerful alle-gory of the dialectic of enlightenment, for Odysseus to hear the Sirens' song, he must be bound to the ship's mast by his deafened sailors.)[4] And while Adorno and Horkheimer perceived the threat of Europe's cultural Americanization, Greenberg and Macdonald were ideologues *of* this Americanization, part of an organized effort to convince the world that American culture was worthy of the United States' status as a superpower—was, in other words, something more exalted than the commercial products of Hollywood and Tin Pan Alley. Indeed, in recognition of the importance of this ideological work, journals like the *Partisan Review* and its new critical counterpart the *Kenyon Review* were secretly funded by the CIA.[5] Thus, while Greenberg championed the American abstract expressionists as the true heirs to the European avant-garde, Macdonald labored to prove that the propagandistic mass culture of the Soviet Union was not only as prevalent as, but of even worse quality than, that of the American culture industry: its movies even "duller and cruder" than Hollywood's, its public architecture more "lunatic," its cultural commentary more "childish."[6]

By the 1980s, an idea of "mass culture" ostensibly built upon Horkheimer and Adorno's views came to refer to a particular kind of object and political position. "Mass culture" delineated the kind of corporate and official culture directed at the passive mass consumer. "Popular culture," on the other hand, became a signal for a more populist Gramsci-inspired perspective that emphasized the formation of political subjectivity, in which the expressive forms emanating from a particular group of people were imagined as the medium through which oppositional politics and identities might emerge. The comparison between these definitions and their implied perspectives typically worked to the detriment of mass culture. In John Fiske's well-known formulation, "Popular culture is made from within and below, not imposed from without or above as mass cultural theorists would have it."[7]

This facile opposition, like the one between art and mass culture, also had a number of distorting effects. For one, it may have seriously mischaracterized the work of figures like Adorno, whose relationship to his mass cultural object was more dialectical than he is often read to be.[8] Similarly, it oversimplified the best cultural studies work, which, at its very core, sought to understand the complex satisfactions and identifications behind various expressive forms of daily life, even the most mass-produced of them. Thus Fredric Jameson—who along with Martin Jay was most responsible for introducing the Frankfurt School to English-speaking readers—famously showed how Hollywood hit movies work on a double political axis: not mere reifications of the status quo, they also hinted at some other "utopian" dimension that alluded to how life could be lived otherwise. Though they were produced by a perhaps cynical culture industry, films like *Jaws* and *The Godfather*, to be successful, had to speak to the deeper unalienated desires of their audience.[9] Likewise, even the most dedicated searchers after authentic pockets of popular cultural expression did so with the alternative firmly in mind: an encroaching and homogenizing global culture that appeared to be wiping out the diversity and originality of human expression.

If Franzen's caricature in *The Corrections* is any guide, it appears that with the passage of time one half of this double stereotype has landed and stuck smack on the reputation of cultural studies as a whole. In that vision, cultural studies was only ever a study of "popular culture": it was only ever about finding subversion and rebellion in small acts, rare tastes, and minutely inscribed identifications. And so, if cultural studies is a dead project, then we might say mass culture is doubly dead: the discarded half of a spurious opposition in a project that in general seems to have outlived its moment.

There is an important clue to the story of mass culture in the quick histories I have offered above: whether addressing mass culture as opposed to art or as opposed to popular culture, they seem largely to be narratives about the 1930s and 1940s in conversation with the 1980s. So what happened in the intervening decades? Quite a lot happened in postwar America that would seem to directly impinge on this topic of mass culture: enormous social phenomena such as the rise of television and mass consumer society; dramatic changes in the structure of social space, including the dispersal of white working- and middle-class communities into suburbia; and over all of it, the ascendance of the United States as the most militarily, politically, and economically powerful nation on earth.[10] Yet it is interesting that in this hugely transformative moment mass culture was not particularly visible, either as a term or as a topic. Instead, midcentury observers largely turned their attention to two somewhat divergent projects: on the one hand, *media* and their social effects; on the other, consumer behavior and the creation of markets. Could it be that mass culture was already dead in 1946? If we are to understand how and why we might still be haunted by mass culture, it's time to return to the scene of the crime.

THE CHARNEL SHIP

One early autumn evening in 1934, the wreck of the steamship *Morro Castle* ran aground off the shore of Asbury Park, New Jersey. The *Morro Castle* was still smoldering from a disastrous fire that had killed 137 persons when, charred remains of the victims still on board, it broke loose from its towline and lodged in the sand an easy swim's distance from the resort town's public city beach. By the next day, crowds of sightseers numbering as many as a quarter of a million, spurred on by print and radio reports of the grounding and special excursion railroad fares from New York and Philadelphia, flocked to the seaside town to view the still-burning shipwreck. The atmosphere was festive around what one contemporary account called "the charnel ship":

> Shouts would go up when a spurt of flame shot from the liner. Many seemed to share the opinion of a fat woman who, after sitting for hours on the damp sand, explained to the girl beside her, "Yeah, I'm tired all right, but I ain't going to see nothing like this for a long time." Boys with baskets of soda pop, hamburgers and pretzels pushed through the crowds. Salesmen hawked photographs of the ship, some of them realistically tinted red to indicate the fire. New York newspapers were in demand because of their excellent aërial pictures of the fire-scarred ship.[11]

The scene at the wreck of the *Morro Castle* was both a spontaneous public festival and a media event. Postcards were printed, souvenirs were sold, and radio broadcasts offered both firsthand accounts of the scene on board the wreck, complete with lurid descriptions of charred corpses, *and* coast-to-coast coverage of a lavish memorial service for the victims of the disaster. An enterprising mother tried to display her infant to best advantage in Coney Island's annual baby parade on a float representing the burned ship (this was deemed in poor taste by the judges, and the child was disqualified from the competition).[12] Meanwhile, the city fathers of Asbury Park planned to "push Atlantic City off the map" by mooring the wreck permanently in place as a tourist attraction.[13] The plan was scrapped only when the ship's cargo of uncured cowhides began to rot and inundated blocks of the city surrounding the beach with an ungodly stench. The ship was eventually towed away to a New York salvage yard.

This anecdote can, I think, serve as a fairly rich example of what might have been meant, in 1939, by mass culture. First, anyone familiar with the literature or cultural history immediately recognizes something familiar in the sheer grotesquerie of this scene. It evokes the brutal riot that ensues from a crowd gathered for a Hollywood movie premiere in Nathanael West's *The Day of the Locust,* or William Carlos Williams's representation of "The Crowd at the Ballgame," "moved uniformly by a spirit of uselessness" inherent in the spectacle they are enjoying, yet ominously capable of thoughtless violence: "it is deadly, terrifying— /It is the Inquisition, the/Revolution."[14] We may think, as well, of the lynch mobs and "Ku Kluxers" of the post–World War I red scare and its aftermath, or of H. L. Mencken's portrayal of the "gaping primates" who descended from the Tennessee hills to hear the "mountebank" William Jennings Bryan rail against evolution.[15] In Asbury Park, there were mountebanks aplenty: the press who covered the event in such sensational detail, the vendors of souvenirs who catered to the public's lurid tastes, and the members of the infrastructure of coastal New Jersey tourism who sought to capitalize on the excitement.

What to make of all this carnivalesque activity? For Michael Warner, this kind of eruption of questionable behavior is inherent in the bourgeois public sphere, which has always posed a social contradiction between the imaginary disembodied (and implicitly white, straight, adult, male, propertied) subject who inhabits that sphere and actual, complexly embodied persons. Mass mediation only serves to heighten and render visible this fundamental contradiction through the often grotesque eruption of the body in, for example, media coverage of gory disasters and tabloid-style fascinations with stars' weight fluctuations and plastic surgeries.[16] Of course, a far older explanation would hold that it is something inherent in the dynamic of crowds. If, as Richard Sennett puts it, "the crowd is man the animal let off his leash," then the animal in question springs from nineteenth-century bourgeois anxieties about urban encounters with potentially dangerous others.[17] These others, the urban underclasses and other frightening sorts, are almost by definition ruled by dangerous passions and impulses. Their unruly passions, as Gustave LeBon famously argued, could then spontaneously spread even to those (middle-class) individuals who normally possessed self-control.[18] This context of class othering, made only more explicit by the neoaristocratic theories of T.S. Eliot and José Ortega y Gasset, explains Raymond Williams's wholesale rejection of the very idea of the masses: "Masses are other people. There are in fact no masses; there are only ways of seeing people as masses. In an urban industrial society there are many opportunities for such ways of seeing."[19]

Despite this baggage, I will retain the idea of the masses provisionally for another reason: its inclusion in the more evaluatively neutral phrase "mass media." For indeed, there does seem to me something qualitatively different about the *Morro Castle* incident. Not simply another example of the grotesque eruption of the passions of the unruly crowd, this case seems distinctive for the way that various crowds—on the beach, on the trains, and at the baby parade—interacted with the mass media.

The media had a hand in bringing the spectators to Asbury Park, but the crowds themselves then also formed spectacles that in turn provoked more, and different kinds of, media participation. The event off the Jersey shore could be experienced vicariously by listeners a continent away, and that in turn surely also made a difference to the behavior of the crowd. Indeed, the presence of the media seems crucial to understanding the distinctive character of an event like this, separating it off analytically from earlier examples of spectacle and sensation. But the presence of the crowd in this mass-mediated extravaganza also indicates a difference between the "ballyhoo years" of emergent mass media and advertising and the postwar moment of its complete consolidation.[20] In other words, this incident, where production and consumption are conspicuously intermingled via the presence of an actively participatory crowd, violates a conventional definition of mass media, which emphasizes the spatial and temporal separation of mass media producers and consumers.[21]

But if we are in the presence of a transitional moment for the mass media, then this incident also represents a changing moment in the popular relationship to social space. Popular entertainments in the early part of the twentieth century revolved around the largely urban spaces of amusement parks, dance halls, movie palaces, parks, and streets.[22] As Theodore Dreiser showed in Sister Carrie, this was also the site of a certain kind of labor. The parade of fashionable people taking the air on Broadway were also checking out the latest in hats and cravats: learning how and what to consume. By the postwar period, however, this world of public entertainment had dramatically changed, so that the very idea of the mass gathering became increasingly rare and largely confined to containable venues such as sports arenas. This was a multicausal transformation, brought on by the promotion of suburban life and an infrastructure dedicated to automobile travel; the ascendance of high modernist architecture, with its disregard for the cityscape; and the transformation of the home by radio and television into a venue for entertainment.[23] Among the multiple consequences of these changes, urban areas began to be considered the site of social problems like poverty and blight, the movie industry went into crisis, and the labor of consumption was much more firmly guided by an ascendant advertising industry. Indeed, the idea of mass media as involving a complete separation between the site of the production of content and the site of reception is also the product of the profound rearrangement of social space that happened after the war. Correspondingly, we can begin to see the between-wars period as distinctive and transitional from a period in which mass-mediated entertainment and the labor of consumption were largely performed in public to one in which these functions were increasingly relegated to the private sphere. In keeping with the terminology of the moment, let us call the transitional between-wars period, when the culture of the crowd and the mass media intersected, *mass culture*.[24]

MASS CULTURE

Examples of this transitionality—the characteristic convergence of new media and spectatorial crowds—are plentiful. Charles Lindbergh's safe return to the United States after his transcontinental flight precipitated a Broadway ticker-tape parade, a public military decoration ceremony on the steps of the Washington Monument, lavish press coverage, and up-to the-minute radio and newsreel reports of it all, beginning before Lindy even reached land.[25] Similarly, the famous Tennessee Scopes trial holds a small place in the history of mass media because a special telephone line was set up by Chicago radio station WGN for an unprecedented live broadcast of the proceedings. But equally remarkable was the carnival atmosphere in Dayton, Tennessee, which actively promoted the trial as a tourist attraction. The small town was filled with spectators, hundreds of reporters, news photographers, and newsreel cameramen, along with itinerant evangelists and atheists hoping to catch the ear of the crowd, souvenir vendors, Bible salesmen, carnival barkers offering glimpses of the "missing link," and photographers who could snap your picture beside a real monkey.[26]

In some ways most telling of the complexity of the moment is the fact that the 1929 stock market crash apparently drew throngs to Wall Street. Though legends persist about speculators jumping to their deaths in the canyons of lower Manhattan at the news of their lost fortunes, there was in fact very little spectacle to greet these crowds. Indeed, as far as transformative historical events go, it is hard to imagine a less spectacular event than a long slow series of downward trending numbers on a ticker tape. Yet it seems that amassing in crowds was how people understood they could participate in what was clearly a momentous occasion, and so they gathered in the place most closely associated with the workings of the markets.[27]

Perhaps the most obvious example of the convergence of crowds and mass media is in the celebrity appearance. One of the earliest star public appearance tours was a drive to sell Liberty Loan bonds during World War I. Not surprisingly, the stars made themselves available primarily to the wealthy potential purchasers of war bonds. But there were also a few exceptionally large crowd appearances. Contemporary estimates ranged as high as one hundred thousand onlookers for a Wall Street appearance by Hollywood's "big three," Charlie Chaplin, Douglas Fairbanks, and Mary Pickford. Though pictures exist of a jolly Chaplin and Fairbanks doing gymnastics in front of their public audience, a slightly more sinister scene greeted Pickford. Mounted police were apparently insufficient to keep back the unruly crowd clamoring to make contact with "America's sweetheart"; it took her forty-five minutes simply to move through the amassed fans to her appointed booth. Later, her megaphone-enhanced public address was completely drowned out by the noise of the crowd, which at times surged menacingly toward the stage. Her panic must have mounted as she shouted futilely for the crowd to hold back. Thenceforth, Pickford is known to have been terrified of public appearances.[28]

Taken together with the story of the burning of the *Morro Castle,* all of these examples should now provide us with some clues as to the grotesque quality of mass culture. Indeed, I would suggest that it is precisely because of mass culture's transitional status in terms of both social space and media penetration that it could be seen as far more chaotic, crass, and carnivalesque than either its predecessors or what would succeed it. Thus what we see in the example of the *Morro Castle* is unregulated crowds meeting up with a largely unregulated (that is to say, developing) mass media. The result is a fairly clear struggle over taste and propriety. We can see signs of the struggle of these various forces in, say, the incident at the baby parade, where the impulses toward publicity and sensation eventually collided with some conception (however rough) of the limits of bad taste. One also imagines that the broadcast of the memorial service for the fire's victims was in some part concocted to counterbalance the more sensational media coverage of the event. In a fully mass-mediated environment, standards of decency would become much more strictly codified to conform to the broadcasters' estimations of what could be tolerated by the broadest swath of its listeners and what would promote their corporate image. Of course, this could be fully achieved only when the crowd was taken out of the picture.

If mass culture represents a transitional moment in the convergence of mass media and public space, then we must also acknowledge some unsettling transitions within the various media involved as well—ones that may well have produced their own grotesque effects. The phenomenon of the star appearance represents one such unsettled site. Early movie companies had no interest in promoting their products via their actors, preferring instead to cultivate brand loyalty to specific studios. But audience interest in their favorite players, combined with the willingness of newspapers and magazines to feed this enthusiasm, overwhelmed the studios' strategy, paving the way for the use of personal appearances for publicity. For the emergent movie industry, however, personal appearances were understood as risky, requiring that the producers balance fans' desires and the benefit of advertising with the perceived need to preserve the star's special qualities as a mass-mediated commodity.[29] This, in turn, offers an important clue to the fans' psychology: the desire to see the screen star in person—perhaps to the extent of physically endangering her—is related to her aura, but not in the Benjaminian sense. The desire to see the star "in the flesh" is the perhaps more aggressive one of penetrating the secret specialness of the mediated image.

Indeed, this desire may be reflective of one that confronts the consumer of any new medium: the desire to locate the line between what is real and what is artifice. With regard to early photography, Alan Trachtenberg has noted that "the process of acclimatization was neither as spontaneous nor as unequivocal as is often assumed."[30] Rather than simply seeing the vast possibilities of mimetic representation offered by the new technology, early observers often found in photography "a confusion of the very elements of nature," in which the fleeting image was now unnaturally fixed.[31] This led to all kinds of speculations about photography's uncanny qualities and about the "theft" of one's likeness, or even one's soul. It also led to phenomena such as the mid-nineteenth-century practice of spirit photography, in which ghostly images of departed loved ones shared the photographic frame with living subjects. These photos purported not only to give evidence of dead loved ones' continued presence on earth but to offer a medium of communication between the living and the dead.[32]

Something similar occurred with the technology of film, which, like photography, opened up whole new possibilities for realistic representation. Early film exhibitions capitalized on film's amazing new powers of representation by showcasing documentary material, and even new breakthroughs in projection technology or other innovations that made the viewing experience as realistic as possible. Of course, as with photography, some explored the new medium's ability to produce magical or uncanny effects. Like the spirit photographers before him, Georges Méliès, in particular, devised a repertoire of techniques to capture supernatural spectacles on film.[33] But the emergence of film as a form that could convey complex narratives came only with the development of a series of other artifices: filming, editing, and acting techniques that enabled identification with characters and the retailing of complex and multiple story lines. Film, as a result, was very early on a hybrid form, simultaneously incorporating both the verisimilitude of the image in motion and the tricks and techniques of effective storytelling.[34] In between these two poles of verisimilitude and artifice was the screen star: a real person, and yet also an actor with a mass-mediated image. Small wonder that the crowd wanted to touch Mary Pickford, to find out what about her was real.

This brings us, inevitably, to radio, the central mass medium of the scene at the *Morro Castle*. No less than photography or film, early radio presented its own uncanny qualities, also related to the problem of discerning the difference between reality and artifice. This, certainly, was an issue as late as 1938, in the famous case of the Mercury Theatre on the Air's broadcast of *War of the Worlds,* which manipulated the established conventions of radio—the news bulletin that interrupts other programming, the on-the-scene reporter—with sufficient dexterity to confuse a sizable portion of its listeners into believing that Martians had landed in New Jersey. Years later, Mercury Theatre's creative genius Orson Welles would frankly acknowledge that behind the broadcast's conception lay a desire to pierce radio's status—or perhaps more precisely, the status of the radio news and information broadcast—as a voice of truth: "We were fed up with the way in which everything that came over this new magic box, the radio, was being swallowed."[35] In this sense, it is possible to see the crowds that swarmed the streets after the *War of the Worlds* broadcast as attempting to reassure themselves of the reality of events experienced via an ambiguously representational medium.

But this is only a partially satisfying explanation of radio's participation in mass culture. By 1938, radio's conventions, and its authority, were sufficiently well established that the real manipulation in the *War of the Worlds* broadcast was not so much of the ambiguities of the medium itself but of its characteristic forms, such as the news bulletin. Rather, to understand radio's uncanny qualities, we must look to its origins as a new technology.

Originally conceived as a device for one-to-one communication, as a telephone-like instrument that was free of the encumbrance of wires, radio's true capacity was soon revealed in what at first seemed its most severe limitation. Unlike a telephone call, a radio broadcast could be overheard by any party with the right equipment, tuned to the right frequency. But this also meant that a radio broadcast could address countless unknown people, an audience, simultaneously. Radio blurred the private space of personal communication and the public space of the mass audience—a mass audience, moreover, that often received the radio transmission in the private confines of the home. As its earlier analysts quickly noted, the radio audience was thus substantively different from that of other mass media, "the congregate group of the moving picture theater and the consociate group reading the daily paper. The radio audience consists essentially of thousands of small, congregate groups united in time and experiencing a common stimulus—altogether making possible the largest grouping of people ever known."[36]

It is in the oscillation of the idea of the "small congregate groups" and "the largest grouping of people ever known"—the confusing collision of private and public—that we find many of the concerns of early commentators about radio as a medium. Many critics bemoaned the loss of a genuine public sphere through radio. Its substantive control in the hands of a few corporate content providers, the inability of listeners to engage with the medium as creators or commentators, the homogenization of content, and the absence of minority voices and perspectives all plausibly seemed to threaten democracy itself.[37] But even more fundamentally, there seemed to be something downright creepy about the way radio insinuated itself into private life, especially the way its noise invaded the solitude of one's home or even one's thoughts. It seemed to require passive consumption and to invite distracted and fragmented listening. Combining these concerns was the specter of the charismatic radio voice: the intimate friend who entered one's living room with the promise of advice, consolation, and a kind of proxy public voice for listeners—that is, to address the very unease listeners may have experienced at the loss of a traditional public sphere. While most famously true of President Roosevelt's extremely effective fireside chats, it was no less so with a host of other more dubious characters, who entered the air often from the fringes of regional radio stations. Especially in the years preceding federal regulation and network consolidation of access to radio frequencies, charismatic radio personalities saturated the airwaves with a common broadcasting formula composed in various parts of entertainment, religion, politics, and medical advice (not unlike the fare currently on offer at televangelist Pat Robertson's Christian Broadcasting Network). These included self-denominated medical experts like Dr. John Brinkley of Kansas, who offered to cure impotence by surgically implanting goat testicles, and hucksters like Iowa's Norman Baker, who used the airwaves, variously, to sell Calliaphones (a musical instrument of his invention), promote dubious cancer cures, and rail against government and corporate control of radio frequencies. It also included the Catholic priest Charles Coughlin, whose radio career began with sermonizing but trended increasingly toward controversial political and economic topics until he was eventually silenced by the church hierarchy.[38]

In a sense, a great many of the charismatic voices of early radio could be seen as partaking of the techniques of fascism simply through the intimacy of their address. As Adorno argued in his analysis of the rhetoric of the evangelist Martin Luther Thomas, the fascist leader's rhetoric "is personal. Not only does it refer to the most immediate interests of his listeners, but it also encompasses the sphere of privacy of the speaker himself who seems to take his listeners into his confidence and to bridge the gap between person and person."[39] Thus the demagogue insinuates himself not only through conventional authoritarianism but through a series of personalizing gestures, portraying himself as a "lone wolf," a "great little man," who cherishes "good old time" values and beliefs and has a humble message to bring to others about the bigger forces that tirelessly persecute him and ultimately endanger the members of his audience and their way of life.[40] Where the medium of radio provokes a certain ambiguity concerning the line between the public and private spheres, the fascist, according to Adorno, explicitly manipulates this ambiguity to promote his political agenda and authority.

A couple of corollaries follow somewhat loosely from this point: that radio is the quintessential fascist medium; that mass culture as a whole is fascist; that the addressee of mass culture is particularly susceptible to fascism, or at least, manipulation. But it is worth pointing out that Adorno, at least, isn't quite saying any of these things. First, Adorno's common point of comparison between the radio evangelist and the fascist leader is formal in nature: his is essentially an argument about rhetoric and performance. Moreover, in most of his work on radio Adorno says very little about the audiences for these broadcasts. Unlike his colleagues at the Princeton Office of Radio Research, who conducted many surveys and interviews with listeners (and thereby pioneered the techniques of market research for the postwar consumer society), Adorno was antipathetic to the project of gathering information on the listening audience. Not only were such interviews and data sets in his view ultimately in the service of the radio broadcasters and advertisers, but they came to represent for Adorno an essential example of instrumental reason.[41] Rather, especially in his work on classical music, Adorno's concerns were focused on a very different problem: the Benjaminian one of the mechanical reproducibility of the work of art. For Adorno, the constraints of the medium of radio and the choices of its broadcasters entailed that what audiences got in the way of classical music was only a vague simulacrum of the experience of a live classical music performance. Worse, under the guise of public-spirited cultural education, classical music programming turned the music into mere "fetishes," signs of taste and distinction, shorn of their actual cultural value and even listening pleasure.[42] His work on radio is, in other words, essentially a theorization of the *medium*—just as much as his influential critique of the culture industry is a critique of the capitalist structure of the dissemination of cultural products and not of its consumers. This is a point often lost when Adorno is taken to be yet another example of the prewar critic of the masses. Rather, one could say that Adorno's emphasis on the media makes him seem more a figure of the debates that characterized the postwar.

All of which brings us back to the crowd—or more specifically, the crowds that massed around in conjunction with a mediated event. While it is easy to assimilate this phenomenon into some specter of fascism, it is clear that events like the crowds on the beach in Asbury Park were not Nuremberg rallies: they were more or less carnivals, spontaneous gatherings of people with very different agendas. But it is possible to read this behavior in light as well of the general confusion between public and private, brought about both by nascent changes in public space and by the features of the radio medium itself. The crowd, in this sense, was a kind of historical artifact of an older organization of public space, vanishing under the pressure of a nascent mass media.

FROM MASS CULTURE TO MEDIA ENVIRONMENT

Now, it is possible to offer another explanation for why I want to reserve for this moment—and no other—the term "mass culture." For it is with the term "culture" that we may register some of these ambivalences and confusions emanating from the emergence of a different historical relationship between the public and the private. This more historically specific usage of "mass culture" will do a few things for us. First, it will help us see not only the transitionality of this moment but its inherent open-endedness: a moment rife with both possibilities and terrors. Second, it will help us to differentiate between the prewar conversations about mass culture and the postwar moment in which concern overwhelmingly turned to the topic of mass media: the form rather than the larger social context.

Much of the prewar critique of mass culture placed the emphasis on the *masses* and their culture (or lack of it). Thus it is in some senses true that debates about mass culture proper are exemplified by neo-aristocrats like José Ortega y Gasset and T.S. Eliot, who took mass culture to be a sign of the decay of civilization and individuality. Mass culture came, for them and many others, to represent a cultural leveling to some common denominator of humanity, with severe consequences to traditional values and individual achievements. But even within this critique, and among the many critics of mass culture from less conservative perspectives, mass culture represented an assault on conventional views of a democratic polity—which is to say, the conventionally conceived public sphere. The grotesque eruptions of violence, mayhem, and vulgarity surrounding mass culture were not (contra Warner) simply examples of a public whose embodied realities exceeded the ideals of this public sphere; they also represented a real attempt to resolve the contradictions of a moment in which the meaning of public space was itself in transition.

Much of this uncertainty was settled after the war. Marshall McLuhan, the most influential of the new media theorists, in some ways wrote the final chapter on mass culture, defining radio as essentially a "private experience" and dismissing the commonplace association between the rise of Hitler and radio-based propaganda as epiphenomenal: an anomalous product of the German "tribal" psyche.[43] His emphasis on the private experience of radio listening was, of course, entirely in keeping with the more general postwar transition away from urban public space to the privatized suburban landscape of the ranch house, the freeway commute, and the shopping mall, where the private sphere and individualism were taken to be the cornerstones of the cold war American way of life. Thus, while popular sociologists like David Riesman and William H. Whyte were fretting over the dangers of social conformity, the advertisers and market researchers began to conceptualize even consumption in increasingly individualized terms. With the emergence of "niche" and "segmented" marketing in the 1960s and 1970s, in which products were targeted to ever more finely drawn subsets of the general population, a writer in *Business Week* opined that the terms "'mass marketing' and 'mass media' have almost become misnomers."[44] As the idea of the masses decayed into the now-familiar pattern of ethnic, gender, age, and income cohorts (a convergence of marketing and sociology that had no small impact on the development of multicultural identity categories), the outrage and moral panic that characterized earlier excoriations of the crowd and the masses would find its new target in specific market segments—especially youth culture, with its proclivity for dangerous styles and media forms like comic books and rock music.[45]

But if the idea of the masses was under revision, there was more intensive focus than ever before on the "media." More relevant to McLuhan than any mechanism of crowd behavior was the nature of radio as a "hot" medium, capable of saturating its passive listeners with information. Indeed, as his famous slogan "The medium is the message" conveys, the new media theory emphasis was almost entirely on the formal capacities of the media. But McLuhan also recognized that the postwar moment of the media, characterized by TV, represented a transformation of social space: a new "environment" saturated not only by television and the perceptual habits it dictated but by a fully privatized, suburbanized imaginative space consonant with postwar social ideals.[46] Much of the popular discourse on media, even at its most critical (Jerry Mander's *Four Arguments against Television*, 1977, or Edward S. Herman and Noam Chomsky's *Manufacturing Consent*, 1988), largely followed suit.

As a challenge to this late modernist consensus, postmodern media critics at once embraced the universality of the mediated environment and interrogated it by in effect pushing the logic of niche marketing to its logical extreme. So conceived, the media consumer was not a passive recipient of the media but one who was fully capable of engaging with it critically, creatively, and even subversively: the teenage mall rat who elaborated ways to waste time in the fully commercial environment of the shopping mall; the minority viewer who developed creative ways to identify with the mass-mediated images that excluded her. But underneath all these celebrations of creativity and détournement of the media environment there remains a consistent sense of unease about the meaning and magnitude of these kinds of gestures. If we are haunted by mass culture, then, it is because of its relationship to the unruly potentiality of the crowd. Mass culture haunts our imagination precisely because it represents the last moment of collective public life before the complete, and seemingly intractable, consolidation of our current configuration of social space.

CHAPTER 3

A Brief History of
the Cultural Turn

To begin this historical account of the cultural turn in the context of the cold war (1946–89), I want to build upon a central point from chapter 1 about the relationship between dialectics and the culture concept with a quasi-definitional proposition. In the broader rhetoric of culture, the term can be seen to serve a specific purpose: namely registering, and sometimes seeming to offer the ideological resolution to, various intractable paradoxes. It is in this sense that "culture" becomes the site of the mediation between part and whole: between individual and society, between the smaller group and the larger group, between the universal and the particular. For a classic example of this, we could turn to Matthew Arnold, for whom the individual pursuit of perfection, which he denominated "culture," also somewhat magically led to the creation of a collective "culture" in the state, which in turn equally magically fostered individuals' "best selves." This was not only circular but a deeply ideological maneuver on Arnold's part, allowing him to imagine a way that individuals might cohere within a nation despite the otherwise violently intractable differences of class, religion, and so forth that characterized his moment.[1] As Herbert Marcuse put it in his critique of the idea of culture, "A realm of apparent unity and apparent freedom was constructed within culture in which the antagonistic relations of existence were supposed to be stabilized and pacified. Culture affirms and conceals the new conditions of social life."[2]

But Marcuse reminds us that the rhetorical field of culture is not mere ideology. As he says of the bourgeois idealism of which culture is a part, "It contains not only the justification of the established form of existence but also the pain of its establishment: not only quiescence about what is, but also remembrance of what could be."[3] In this sense culture also marks the space of the resolution of another imaginary contradiction: between the way things are and our more utopian desires. Marcuse here offers a useful gloss to my narrative of mass culture as a transitional moment between a pre-mass-mediated form of existence lived out in public space and that of a fully mass-mediated and privatized daily life. The complex affective states produced by mass culture—including the creepy grotesquerie that sometimes surrounds it—are nothing less than the historical residue of these changes: the pain of their establishment and the missed opportunities they displaced.

In turning, then, to the cold war period, the task at hand is to determine the nature of the paradoxes that culture seemed to help resolve in the postwar twentieth century. This, in turn, will help us to understand the reason for the cultural turn of the late 1980s and 1990s.

A certain version of the immediate postwar years might suggest a general antipathy to the idea of culture. In addition to the displacement of "mass culture" by a formal emphasis on the mass media, this was a moment characterized in the international political arena by an orientation not to cultural specificity but to a universalizing concern with human rights.[4] Moreover, in this high moment of the New York Intellectuals and the literary New Critics, their similar projects of rescuing art from the contaminating questions of context (politics, history, and daily life) can be interpreted as hostility to "culture" and culturalist thinking.[5] And yet, as a number of important critical voices have demonstrated, "culture" was a central and abiding keyword of the postwar twentieth century.

One such text to make this case is Michael Denning's *Culture in the Age of Three Worlds*.[6] For Denning, "culture" is a catch-all term not only for cultural studies and academic work in mass media and communications but for many of the more transformative intellectual developments of the postwar world, including poststructuralist and postcolonial theory. All of these he ties to a global rise of various New Lefts, which, whether in Birmingham, Brazil, or India, attributed a new significance and urgency to those elements of contemporary daily life that an older Left had often dismissed as merely superstructural.[7] But what also emerges in Denning's history of the "age of three worlds" is a nascent discourse of what will finally come to be understood as globalization. Culture (or rather, all these interrelated strains of discourse yoked together under the name "culture") thus figures for him as a kind of vanishing mediator, a way of registering the antinomies of a globalizing world before we were fully historically able to develop a new discourse for it.

In this sense, Denning's work is another contribution to the literature explaining why we are now "beyond culture." I would thus challenge his temptation to see globalization as the final realization of a new order that ultimately makes culture obsolete. Nevertheless, his effort to historicize the cultural turn is important to my argument, and I take his periodization seriously, for it does seem to me that the postwar period marked a new moment in cultural discourse and that his ending point of 1989 represents a historical transition of such significance that I must at least give some account of its effects.[8] Denning might be faulted for neglecting the prewar, modernist, moment, which I see as the crucial site of the formation of the modern culture concept.[9] But I think this avoidance of the genealogical has the advantage of allowing us to focus on culture in a different way: to consider the postwar period as the moment of the culture concept's greatest impact and then to ask to ask why this happened.

In his introduction to his classic work *Keywords* (1976), Raymond Williams offers an interesting anecdote that serves as an origin story for his long and productive engagement with "culture"—an engagement, moreover, that perhaps best demonstrates "culture's" centrality to twentieth-century thought. There, Williams relates the story of how he returned to Cambridge after service in World War II, only to sense that the very acts of thinking and speaking about the world seemed to have profoundly changed. These changes bought home to Williams the complexity and historical contingency of language in general but crystallized most clearly around his sense of a dramatically altered usage of what would become his most famous keyword "culture." Williams noticed that whereas before the war the term had connoted an area of refinement and high feeling, it now carried a new, more capacious meaning of a whole way of life.[10]

This was the generative insight that ultimately led to his explication of the basic contradictions that have hovered around the term: especially the convergence of the real and the ideal, the universal and the particular.[11] But Williams's founding insight into culture's complexity also has a specific historical context, for he notes in passing that this new meaning of culture was *American* in origin. As a purely philological point, Williams was here registering the fact that this usage of culture as a whole way of life was a popular British adoption of American social scientific usages of "culture." These included usages common in various kinds of sociology and market research, as well as in "culture-and-personality" anthropology, a dominant school of applied anthropology during wartime and in the early cold war years. Made famous by such works as Ruth Benedict's study *The Chrysanthemum and the Sword: Patterns of Japanese Culture* (1946), culture-and-personality approaches would be heavily employed by the postwar U.S. government as a form of quasi-intelligence, especially on the increasingly inscrutable and threatening "personality" of the Soviet enemy.[12] But in the context of the United States' heavy involvement in postwar reconstruction, western Europe was also subjected to this school of cultural theorization, as well as to American-style social scientific marketing and surveying techniques.[13] In retrospect, then, this American influence on "culture's" older meaning in Britain also signals the enormous changes sweeping over Europe in the postwar period, the decisive moment of American political, economic, and, yes, *cultural* ascendancy.[14]

In other words, what Williams noted in his founding philological observation was also a rhetorical artifact of the nascent American century, the product of a kind of linguistic Marshall Plan. Indeed, if we were to read postwar Americanization as the subtext of Williams's long fascination with culture, then his response is also telling. For what Williams essentially did in works such as *Culture and Society* (1958) was to repatriate culture, situating it firmly within British intellectual traditions. This move would both suture his work to other contemporary studies of British daily life by E. P. Thompson and James Hoggart and in time, precisely because of its more narrowly national emphasis, turn Williams and this work into something of a vanishing mediator for the more globally focused kind of scholarship that would soon come under the name of British cultural studies.[15]

Meanwhile, culture remained central to the rhetorical struggle to suture a new international order under U.S. leadership. This struggle was played out in the context of one very specific contradiction: that which obtained between universalism and particularism. This contradiction between local and national particularism and human universalism emanates very much from the context of responses to Nazism. The United States' own very strong culturalist tradition in the 1930s was significantly challenged by the perceived imperative of countering

Nazi claims to a unique social and political destiny for Germany and its mythical Aryans. Notoriously, such culturalist arguments were used to justify not only the annexation of ethnically German parts of Czechoslovakia and Poland but genocide itself. Moral universalism—the proposition that there are fundamental common moral issues upon which all of humanity agrees—thus became foundational to the political thinking of the World War II period and carried over into the basic contours of American cold war ideology.[16] Indeed, to the distress of such political pragmatists as George F. Kennan, a major architect of U.S. foreign policy in the early cold war, universalism had if anything *excessively* captivated U.S. public opinion, causing many to forget "the national peculiarities and diverging political philosophies of foreign peoples": that is to say, the "ugly realities" of the new cold war world. Such "escapism," he thought, was embodied in institutions like the United Nations and UNESCO.[17]

Yet organizations like UNESCO (United Nations Educational, Scientific, and Cultural Organization) could also be said to have presented a uniquely *cultural* response to the problems of fascism, cold war conflict, and ultimately that great problem of the global order of the three worlds: development. Formed in 1946 on the oft-repeated proposition that "since wars begin in the minds of men, it is in the minds of men that the defenses of peace must be constructed," UNESCO stood for the proposition that mutual awareness, understanding, and communication across cultural differences would lead to tolerance and thence to peace. In other words, cultural differences were not so strong as to limit the possibility of mutual understanding. Moreover, any cultural difference was framed within a context of "humanity," which expressed not only a universal commonality but a set of moral limits to expressions of cultural difference. The early rhetoric of UNESCO is rife with this basic contradiction: "Channels for the free flow of ideas cannot and should not be used to promote a uniform world culture. UNESCO's goal is rather unity-in-diversity; to aid in using these channels so that one culture can be interpreted to other cultures; so that men can learn first those common elements in the other culture that can serve as the basis for common thought and action; but, of equal importance, that they may learn respect for other divergent elements."[18]

Because UNESCO's founding impulses (put forth by such important early figures as Julian Huxley, Stephen Spender, and André Malraux) were those of a European antitotalitarian liberalism, the fear expressed in the UNESCO document of a "uniform world culture" was directed equally to the perceived global ambitions of the United States and the Soviet Union. From the perspective of the United States, the goal was never explicitly "Coca-colonization" (though foreign markets were certainly opened to U.S.-based corporations) but rather the global propagation of a positive and potentially emulative appreciation for the "American way of life." In other words, U.S. cold war propaganda perfectly replicated the contradiction at the heart of UNESCO cultural theory. The proposition, quite simply, was that the United States had a democratic culture distinctive to it, the likes of which not only would be universally admired but should "serve as the basis for common thought and action." This was a guiding premise of what would come to be "three worlds" theory, in which the aspirations of the "third world" were understood to be identical with U.S.-style capitalist democracy. It was also the obvious message of much of the work of Marshall Plan institutions like the America Houses, which quite impressively carried out their mission to be "outposts of American culture" in Europe, with concerts, plays, films, and libraries full of books by American creators—the working assumption being that a taste for Hemingway, Gershwin, and O'Neill would also, viruslike, impart an inclination toward American-style political and economic structures. If, as Serge Guilbaut memorably put it, the United States "stole" the idea of modern art from Europe, what it sent back was American culture.[19]

Meanwhile, even as the United States presented itself to the cold war world as the simultaneously unique and universal world culture of the future, culture was operating in a somewhat different register on another front, in the United States' domestic War on Poverty. Here, the operative cultural language was that of the "culture of poverty." Another outgrowth of culture-and-personality anthropology, the term had been coined by Benedict's student, Oscar Lewis, in his *Five Families: A Mexican Case Study in the Culture of Poverty,* a set of five ethnographies linked together to address the transition of Mexican peasants into the urban lumpen proletariat.[20] The phrase was quickly applied to African Americans, whose situation seemed especially to represent what was widely seen as the "paradox" of poverty in the affluent postwar United States. In the work of Nathan Glazer and Daniel Patrick Moynihan, the idea of a "culture of poverty" converged with the pioneering work of Chicago School sociologist E. Franklin Frazier, whose classic studies of the 1930s focused on issues like illegitimacy and family abandonment in black communities.[21] The "culture of poverty" idea then became a way not only to suggest that the conditions of poverty were due to characteristic behaviors of the poor themselves but, in Moynihan's role as an important formulator of federal policy, to deflect official attention from the demands arising from the civil rights movement—issues such as voting rights and employment opportunities—onto the "fundamental problem" of black "family structure."[22]

But I want to look more specifically at the grounds from which this position was critiqued, notably by Charles A. Valentine, in his 1968 book *Culture and Poverty*. For Valentine, the "culture of poverty" thesis had two flaws: in addition to blaming the victim and being fundamentally tautological (the poor are poor because they are not middle class), it represented poor cultural theory. The idea of the culture of poverty tended for him to misapprehend an anthropological conception of culture in some basic ways, for example by confusing culture with class and by assuming that "culture" connoted a homogeneous and unchanging set of behaviors and attitudes. More generally, it inadequately addressed the central anthropological question about how to resolve the tension between particularism and universalism—in this case, by failing to explain how the local conditions and views of the impoverished were related to larger social, political, and economic forces. Lewis, for example, came in for criticism for not offering a convincing account of how his subject families and individuals were representative of the kinds of larger patterns that he attributed to them. But the complaint about the thesis's determinism is indicative of another realm of cultural thinking, the one that attempts some resolution between real and ideal. Here, indeed, a determinist "culture of poverty" not only failed to resolve the problem of real and ideal but offered a kind of negative inverse of that project: a vision of culture as the central mechanism of how life ought *not* to be. Rather than suturing the conflict between the real and the ideal, the "culture of poverty" idea occupied the space of the conflict between the descriptive and the determinative. I would argue that the idea of the culture of poverty thus failed not only on the grounds of widespread antipathy to what were understood to be its political implications but as an example of cultural theory.

Put another way, the problem with the culture of poverty idea was that it took as its premise the exception of poverty within the United States; poverty was part of some "other America."[23] So there was no position from which to see the culture of poverty as being in any way related to some larger American culture, or some other economic or social structure. There was no way, as well, to use the idea of a culture of poverty to critique the dominant society, or to use its realities to imagine a more ideal situation. Unfortunately, this has only been exacerbated in recent decades of poverty theory, as features of the culture of poverty idea have taken hold, and as poverty has been increasingly pathologized, in the age of welfare "reform."[24] But then, we can see similar limitations to the cold war ideology of American culture as well. In the cold war arena, anything that deviated from the universal human aspirations that went under the name of "America," such as Soviet communism, was similarly an unaccountable aberration: an embodiment of evil, a "system of total error."[25] Such an aberration could offer no point from which this American culture could be critiqued. No wonder so many intellectuals found midcentury cultural rhetoric to be stultifying.

Thus far, I have shown how cultural theory may have resolved certain paradoxes (and how unsuccessful cultural theory failed to offer such resolutions), but I have offered nothing in the way of a helpful genealogical key for thinking about the impressive explosion of cultural theory in the 1980s and 1990s. Indeed, the inadequacy of ideas like the culture of poverty helps to explain why many scholars in the social scientists and humanities in the mid–twentieth century remained relatively unimpressed by the idea of culture and instead moved toward such universalizing modes of thought as structuralism. So what happened to change this picture? To answer this question, we must turn to what we might see as a countertradition of midcentury intellectual life—indeed to a counterculture: the significant convergence of new intellectual and social forces in the notorious period that often goes by the date 1968.

According to Giovanni Arrighi, Terence Hopkins, and Immanuel Wallerstein, 1968 marks the emergence of wholly new kinds of social movements. These included Maoist movements; student, labor, and antiwar movements; movements of liberation based on ethnic, racial, gender, and sexual identity; environmentalism; human rights movements; and most recently, antiglobalization and antineoliberalism movements. Significantly for these writers, all of these newer kinds of movements represented an important shift in the political imaginary, in which the nationalist elements that had been so prevalent in the antisystemic struggles of the past were to varying degrees discarded. What the newer movements instead emphasized was allegiance with the oppressed—ethnic and racial minorities, the poor, the people of the developing world, women, sexual minorities, and so forth.[26]

Of course, "1968" here stands for the culmination of a trend of events that had begun in the previous decades of the postwar period, including the emergence of movements of postcolonial liberation and civil rights in the United States. What changed their character, however, was the escalation of the Vietnam War: a struggle between vastly unmatched national powers; between imperial forces and the barely postcolonial periphery; between poorly armed guerillas and a massive industrialized military. Moreover, as Arrighi, Hopkins, and Wallerstein explain it, the war's escalation threatened the lives and futures of American, Chinese, and of course Vietnamese youth, as well as (because of the resulting global monetary crisis) the economic security of European youth and workers. Meanwhile, these same groups were beginning to feel the full ideological impact of the civil rights movement, the Chinese Cultural Revolution, and the postcolonial movements of independence. "Taken together, all these movements and their Vietnamese epicenter were important in disclosing a basic asymmetry in the power of systemic and antisystemic forces on a world scale."[27] The result was not only a surge in the activism of antisystemic movements but activism that eschewed national models of global order in favor of identifications with subalternity.[28]

As we all know, students were the actual catalysts of many of the struggles of this period, and schools—particularly in the dramatically enlarged and democratized postwar universities of the United States—were significant sites of these struggles. Indeed, in the United States especially, universities were increasingly the institutional home of intellectuals, and thus their context alone demanded that intellectuals respond to these events one way or another. Those who already possessed liberal-left sentiments of a classic nationalist kind now shifted their attitudes somewhat to conform to the new postnational shape of the important antisystemic movements of the period. This is the kernel of substance behind the accusations of lack of patriotism that are to this day still occasionally lobbed at the scholarly generation of 1968 (a topic I will expand on in chapter 4). But to put these changes in more positive terms, one of the significant victories of the generation of 1968 is that it is no longer possible for scholars and intellectuals in the humanities and social sciences of any political stripe to ignore such vectors of human analysis as gender, race, and sexuality. These kinds of considerations, for example, dragged literary studies out of formalism and the study of American history out of consensualism.

Moreover, this general realignment of academic concerns encouraged a fascination for theoretical perspectives that offered new ways to think about such problems as ideology, subjectivity, power, and subordination, and these in turn significantly challenged structuralism. This is thus the moment of the Anglo-American academy's discovery not only of the western Marxists (Adorno, Lukács, Althusser, Macherey, Gramsci, Benjamin) but of Jacques Lacan's revisions of Freud, Michel Foucault's analysis of the operations of power, and Jacques Derrida's startling challenges to the Western philosophical tradition. As Antony Easthope put it in his tellingly titled history *British Post-Structuralism: Since 1968,* "Structuralism becomes transformed into post-structuralism when the structures of the text are seen to be always structures in and for a subject."[29] That is, these many currents of poststructuralist thinking emanated from 1968, in the necessity to now locate within one's frames of analysis the specific positions and subjectivities of all those who could no longer be regarded as the people without history.

In this very limited historical sense, the right-wing culture warriors of the 1980s and early 1990s weren't entirely wrong when they lumped together into an unholy jumble of depravity all the academic "isms" that they could think of (if not necessarily understand): feminism, Marxism, poststructuralism, postmodernism, multiculturalism, Afrocentrism, postcolonialism, and so on.[30] But to make a list such as this is to immediately see a greater irony within this intellectual sea change that began in the 1960s. Though all these various movements and their adherents were generally in some kind of political alliance—I would be tempted to say they shared a post-1968 habitus—this was often an uneasy coalition indeed. First, of course, the political aims and emphases among the various kinds of feminists and Marxists and scholars with a multitude of other various identitarian interests were sometimes vastly different. But more fundamentally, poststructuralist theory, as a set of insights that often destabilized conventional categories of thought, could be seen to disrupt some of the foundational assumptions of identity-based political movements. Institutionally, we have seen this conflict enacted in war-torn women's studies and ethnic studies programs, riven over conflicts (often heightened by disciplinary differences) between those who were influenced by "theory" and those who claimed some kind of unmediated or realist relationship to their object of study. The conflict between identity and theory can also be summed up in the following complaint, articulated and echoed in various sites since the 1980s: "Just when I've achieved a position of modest power, just when I've acquired a voice that is authorized to speak, you tell me that this position is socially or linguistically constructed!"

This complaint seemed compelling precisely because of the way it brought the intellectual challenges of poststructuralism up short against the general academic habitus of political allegiance with the subaltern. But this is in no way to say that this conflict represented only a dead end of antagonism and guilt. Jane Gallop has argued that the central problem for U.S. academic feminists "around 1981" became one of coming up with some kind of theoretical resolution to the potential space separating feminism (and perhaps especially feminist literary criticism as practiced in the United States) from the insights and challenges of "theory."[31] The conversation between poststructuralist theory, Lacanian psychoanalysis, and feminist politics was both particularly intense and remarkably fruitful, producing lasting insights into the nature and construction of gendered subjectivity. Importantly for my argument, Gallop also notes that at the crest of this wave of feminist theory (sometime in the late 1980s), the issue of race began to come to the fore of feminist work. Though Gallop reads this as an "anxious non-encounter" with the occasionally awkward fact of feminist theory's academic legitimation, it also represents the mechanism by which the creative encounter between identity and theory was potentially endlessly extended.[32]

Indeed, I would argue that this basic conflict between theory and identity holds the key to understanding the cultural turn, for the rhetorical field of "culture" became in this moment the terrain for addressing this general contradiction. The very term "multiculturalism" suggests something of how culture stood on the site of the uneasy meeting between these two registers. On the one hand, "multiculturalism" implied a kind of federation of different subaltern identitarian groups. On the other hand, it quickly entailed a discussion of the multiple registers upon which identity was experienced—not simply in the mixed identities of multiracial individuals but in the way that other vectors such as gender, class, sexuality, region, religion, language, and so forth shot through and complicated all identities. In other words, even at their least theoretical, identitarian studies were pressured by some of the basic insights of poststructuralism regarding subjectivity, social construction, language, and power. Those who argue that "culture" was never anything more than a code word for race are, after all, being self-consciously scandalous precisely because a terminological preference for "culture" over "race" rhetorically signaled a recognition of the very questions that tended to complicate stable conceptions of identity. But what still gives their arguments some play is the widespread sense that the fundamental "cultural" problem of finding a philosophically adequate meeting point between poststructuralist and identitarian positions was never satisfyingly arrived at. Culture in this sense served as a sign of a problem, rather than as a coherent theory itself.

Cultural studies, the area most quickly identified with the cultural turn, is similarly embedded in this contradiction between identity and theory. Indeed, its origins and subsequent development as a field could all be charted as a series of negotiations of this central problem. Cultural studies as a discipline was founded in the red brick of Birmingham in 1964 with an explicit New Left emphasis on working-class culture. But according to at least one recent historian of cultural studies, its real emergence and efflorescence happened only when this object of inquiry met up with a consolidating theoretical perspective—a perspective provided by the "wide-ranging challenges to the epistemological foundations and institutional structures of knowledge production that accompanied the world-scale assault on the liberal consensus by women, colonial subjects, and people of color at the core of the events of 1968."[33] In this case the perspective was first and foremost Althusserian Marxism, which, though still properly structuralist, nevertheless contained several important poststructuralist emphases, including a decentering of historical time, the discursive construction of knowledge, and the social construction of the subject.[34] From this meeting of theory and object emerged the famous extended conflict between Althusserian structuralists and the so-called culturalists, or between (in the eyes of one camp) a bloodless posthumanist theory and (in the eyes of the other) a too-concrete historicism whose analysis stopped with an intense focus on the lives of the oppressed.[35] As in the case of academic feminism, this initial collision of theory and identity (or in this case, subjectivity) would only start waves of other such engagements as cultural studies expanded its purview into issues of race and gender oppression and its geographical range to the United States and Australia.

While it is possible to say that cultural studies as a whole operated on, and gained its relevance from, the terrain of this general conflict, we can also see numerous specific examples of how cultural studies scholars addressed this crisis of a discipline-in-formation. For example, we could account for the success of a book like Dick Hebdige's *Subculture: The Meaning of Style* (1979) precisely on the grounds of its satisfying negotiation of this problem. Hebdige's resolution resided not only in its mix of theory, history, and ethnography but in the particular set of theories he deployed and in his canny emphasis on style as the central site of critical interpretation. The book opens with a lightning-quick tour of cultural studies theory, "from culture to hegemony," which replicates the field's development from Williams's *Culture and Society,* through Roland Barthes' *Mythologies* and Althusser on ideology, to rest finally with Gramsci's discussion of hegemony, "which provides the most adequate account of how dominance is sustained in advanced capitalist societies."[36] There is thus a telos in this trajectory toward Gramsci, one that has often been taken up by those looking for an alternative to Althusser's bloodlessness. But Hebdige's really powerful move was to show how hegemony, itself a system of signs, could be indirectly challenged through the elaboration of subcultural styles. For him, of course, punk would become the quintessential example, and indeed it has become something of the privileged object of British cultural studies generally. But more importantly, this particular conjunction of a general theory of social dominance with an account of specific practices of resistance would come to define the agenda—and the genre—of much of cultural studies research for the next decade.

In any account of the cultural turn, a few other sites must be addressed: the "new cultural history" and the literary new historicism, two fields united most obviously by their common debt to the work of anthropologist Clifford Geertz. In many respects, the story of the new cultural history replicates the pattern I have been developing. French historian Lynn Hunt offers us a narrative of the new cultural history that begins in the 1960s and 1970s with two different emerging trends: a Left-inspired "history from below" and the Annales school. As with Althusser in the case of British cultural studies, Michel Foucault here serves the role of the figure mediating between the structural-functionalism of Annales and more poststructuralist interrogations of subjectivity. In this contested space, Geertz emerges (often as a stand-in for anthropology) precisely because his work is seen to mediate questions of social structure (read, theory) with the local perspective of individual actors.[37] Hunt cites fellow French historian Robert Darnton as follows: "The anthropological mode of history . . . begins from the premise that individual expression takes place within a general idiom."[38] Therefore, the deciphering of meaning in cultural context becomes the central task of the historian, just as Geertz had proposed for anthropology. Similarly, for Stephen Greenblatt, also deeply immersed in Foucault, Geertz offered "the touch of the real" and a way to imagine how, shamanistically, to make the dead voices of the English Renaissance speak again.[39] That is, very much like the historians, he took up the Geertzian project of interpreting meaning within its context.

Insofar as this project served to resituate the centrality of ultracanonical figures like Shakespeare or Dickens, the new historicism can be seen as a reaction to the post-1968 trend in literary studies toward the inclusion of a greater range of figures from previously excluded traditions.[40] Indeed, in many respects the new historicism now seems like a conservative anomaly in the cultural turn. Like cultural studies, the new historicism adopted a central Foucaultian problematic of the relationship of power to subversion. But while in cultural studies the emphasis was on how subcultural or minority groups made meanings in relation to dominant views as a method of creating group solidarity, often for the purposes of creating the subjectivities that made political action, the new historicism often plotted a deeply antiradical narrative in which elements of "subversion" were always already recontained within the larger theatrics of power. Indeed, as Vincent Pecora has noted, the classic new historicist narrative of "contained subversion" neatly reflected the cold war "global theater of competing interests and proxy (that is, symbolic, 'contained,' staged) wars."[41] Yet in some ways new historicism's conservatism can be seen to be the exception that proves the rule about the dominance of the post-1968 academic habitus. First, the very emphasis on "subversion" prevented any easy categorization of new historicism as politically conservative. Moreover, we can now read Greenblatt's famous analogy between literary criticism and shamanism as, among other things, a canny appropriation of exotic alterity for himself and the world he studied. The literary canon, in other words, was preserved precisely by turning both the critic and his texts into subalterns.

Anthropology, the discipline that has had the most sustained encounter with both the culture concept and the subaltern as an object of study, was at the crux of the cultural turn for a very clear reason: it was perceived as the discipline most intimately embroiled in the conflict between theory and identity. The cultural turn in anthropology emerged in the context of what James Clifford referred to in his introduction to the landmark volume *Writing Culture* as the "space opened up by the disintegration of 'Man' as *telos* for a whole discipline"[42]—that is, in poststructuralism's corrosive encounter with the traditional object of study of anthropology itself. But rather than witnessing the dissolution of the discipline, *Writing Culture* reconfigured anthropology in terms of new practices, especially writing and ethnographic practices, which often attempted to address, or at least foreground, some of the relations of power in the ethnographic encounter. In other words, this significant response to the challenge that poststructuralism presented to anthropology involved an intense turn toward the post-1968 scholarly habitus of solidarity with the subalterns who were also anthropology's traditional objects, even at significant expense to the discipline's traditional grounds of authority. Thus, in the name of both interrogating the scene of production of knowledge about the other and offering in its place a picture of the agency and creativity of the ethnographic subject, much of the characteristic work of this moment of "culturalist" anthropology was corrosive of the discipline's more cherished ideas—including, as I have already argued, the culture concept itself.

In sum, then, there was a logic to the success of "culture" as the keyword for a particular trend in scholarly work. Culture became the rhetorical field within which various different kinds of scholars imagined the resolution to what seemed like the most pressing intellectual problem of their moment: the contradiction between theory and identity or subjectivity. If culture no longer seems to be such a central term, what we now need to ask is, Why does this logic no longer seem to hold?

Certainly the answer to this is not that we have successfully resolved the contradiction between theory and identity, for at its most basic level it is irresolvable. Rather, it is that this problem now seems less pressing, less demanding of our time and interest. There are plenty of people out there who are ready to argue that poststructuralism is a dead letter, just as there have always been those who felt that too much time was spent worrying over categories like race and gender. According to this line of thinking, the problem of the cultural turn was already a false one, the product of false suppositions about the radicality or transformative possibilities of this or that starting proposition. Or perhaps we can be more generous, and with Denning suggest a historical end of the cultural turn: we've all simply moved on. In this view, the cultural turn, like postmodernism itself, was a kind of warm-up act to a moment in which we would be more fully able to comprehend our global present. But I think if we are going to historicize, we can do a bit more than saying that the world has changed and academic terminology along with it. Here I'll return to Jane Gallop's history of academic feminism. For Gallop, the moment of the encounter between academic feminist literary criticism and French theory was not only, or even primarily, a sorting out of the political and intellectual impulses emerging from 1968. For her, it was also part and parcel of the institutionalization of feminism within the American literary academy (and with Gallop, I resolutely reject an exclusively negative understanding of academicization). The two forces coming together "around 1981" both helped to establish feminist literary studies as a legitimate field of scholarship. The literary historical focus on the recovery and celebration of women authors opened a space within the academy for feminist concerns, while French feminist theory "rode in on the coattails of the quick rise of deconstruction in American English Studies" to provide academic feminism with intellectual seriousness and a claim to something more than local significance.[43] I think this point can be extended with only minor variation to many of the other areas I have discussed. Certainly this issue of institutional legitimization is a factor in the history of many ethnic studies areas and even of cultural studies, whose moments of formation and theoretical elaboration often followed in quick succession. Conversely, one might be tempted to argue that cultural studies' problem in getting itself a real institutional foothold in the United States was that it never really had a moment in which it carved out a strong niche—say, around a group of texts, or a population like the working class—in the context of an established field. For this reason it retains the status largely of a "method," often taught, as it is in my home department, under the purview of "theory." As for anthropology, it was of course already an established discipline, but one undergoing a serious and self-conscious crisis. As I've already suggested, many strains of the anthropological variant of the cultural turn were an attempt to recreate the discipline's reasons for existence, and I would similarly observe that much of the recent spate of writing for or against culture is continuing to serve a similar function.

So another explanation for the end of the cultural turn must surely have something to do with this issue of academicization. For indeed, other forces were at work around 1981 that ultimately led to a long and largely global period of retrenchment of support for an expanded system of widely accessible universities, and hence to a curtailment in this general project of the creation and expansion of academic fields. First in Thatcher's Britain, then in the United States and elsewhere, universities fell under the same kinds of neoliberal pressures for privatization and fiscal accountability that have for the past twenty-five years affected every part of public life, from welfare to the penal system and the military.[44] In the context of higher education, this withdrawal of public support has largely been in the service of making universities conform to the needs, interests, and models of performance of the corporate sector.[45] For a variety of reasons ranging from the fiscal (we aren't perceived as bringing in self-supporting quantities of grant money or producing profit-generating properties for our institutions) to the political (we are often perceived as the "troublesome" faculty, more likely to participate actively in university "shared" governance or to raise "culture wars"–style public relations problems) to the ideological (we are "tenured radicals," polluting the minds of the young and turning our backs on Shakespeare, patriotism, and truth), scholars in the humanities and interpretive social sciences have been particularly hard hit by this long period of retrenchment. In this climate many of us are encountering new institutional imperatives to justify our very existence within the corporate university, and as such it has real effects on both our rhetorics and the problems that we define as central to our thinking. The end of the cultural turn, in other words, represents the end of the moment in which various energies of the sixties found their home in the American academy.

So this brief history of the cultural turn is an academic story after all. But it is one that shows centrally how the academic discourse has always been in dialogue with the larger concerns and trends of its historical moment. What we should be asking ourselves about now is the extent to which this current moment of disciplinary retrenchment is in fact a disturbing instance of our participation in larger processes of instrumentalization (of knowledge and education, among other things) associated with the post–cold war rise of neoliberalism.

For indeed, if the corollary to the end of the cultural turn is a spate of programmatic calls for return to some of the themes of scholarship in the midcentury—aesthetics, ethics, cosmopolitanism, close reading, and so forth—it is not so much a real return as a return to what feel like historical verities in an attempt to respond to the new conditions in which we find ourselves. The recent rise of academic interest in professional ethics (medical ethics, legal ethics, business ethics, etc.) represents a clear response to precisely the kind of demand now being made on the university in the context of neoliberalism. As Alain Badiou has argued in his philosophical critique of ethics, the purpose of professional ethics is to offer generalized rationalizations for how to manage scarcity, or to cut costs.[46] Professional ethics as a field, in other words, provides research and ideological support for the corporate sector. But for many of these manifestos, the aim seems a more or less futile attempt to tinker with the predominant ideological justifications for our existence: yes, we do "close reading," and care about beauty, and teach the young to be good (and no, we don't muck around in politics or perversion).[47]

But there is another, more classed, way to read some of these returns, for, after all, one of the things that neoliberalism represents is a global moment of intensified class division.[48] And here the new returners seem most akin to their predecessors, the upper-class and conservative New Critics, whose desire was to develop methods of reading that rescued language itself from the reifications of the marketplace. Theirs was, in other words, a response, in retreat, to what they (and many others) saw as the coarsening influence of mass-mediated corporate culture. One could read the current attraction to aesthetics (and "close reading") as a similar kind of retreat from the instrumentalizations of the neoliberal present. Of course, such a response is easier for those in some institutional settings than others: those sheltered from the rationalizations of much of the academy by a largely hereditary role in service to the elite. From such sites of real or imagined privilege, it must now make a kind of sense (as it did in the fifties) to just duck and cover.

CHAPTER 4

Globalization, Culture, and Crises of Disciplinarity

In the decade preceding the turn of the millennium, a spate of pro-grammatic arguments appeared (by, among others, Jane Desmond and Virginia Dominguez, Carolyn Porter, John Carlos Rowe, Priscilla Wald, and José David Saldívar) that called upon Americanists to rethink their field of study in terms of border crossings, transnationalist investiga-tions, and comparatist perspectives. Drawing on scholarship in ethnic studies, feminist and queer studies, postcolonial studies, and even new work in cultural geography, these positions registered a desire to make American studies more reflective not only of the diversity internal to the United States but of the geopolitical context of the late nineties, in which political borders seemed somehow newly friable and the United States seemed both much more closely part, and composed of, a global community.[1]

It should be uncontroversial at this point to suggest that such an act of disciplinary renovation and revision was part and parcel of the cultural turn—indeed, in its postnational critique it was in some ways exemplary of it. And yet, because the object of American studies is ostensibly a national one, this postnationalism presented some particularly acute problems. These problems, in turn, speak especially to the disciplinary features of the cultural turn and help illuminate the consequences of the history outlined in the previous chapter. For the debate around some of the proposals to renovate our understand-ing of the object and methods of American studies proved especially rancorous. For some, the very project of interrogating the national object was a sign of betrayal—if not of the United States as a national formation, than of earlier generations of Americanist scholars for whom, it was suggested, "America" had a deeper, more positive, affective charge. In this argument (let's call it the "love it or leave it" critique), it was alleged that the revisionists ignored the fact that "America" as a concept has important symbolic weight, connoting social and political equality, and indeed the Enlightenment values that undergird any call for social justice. On the other hand—and on this issue most of the revisionists were acutely sensitive—the decentralization of "America" could in fact be its own kind of imperialism in that it markedly extends the purview of American studies into other areas. If, therefore, some would rather that Americanists show some loyalty and "love it or leave it," a critique also exists from a very different political perspective; let's call it the "Yankee go home" problem. While the affective appeals of the "love it or leave it" position were miles apart from the "Yankee go home" critiques, I think they nevertheless both illuminate the problems embedded in the academic context of the cultural turn.

LOVE IT OR LEAVE IT

In 2003, sociologist Alan Wolfe published a review in the pages of the *New Republic* with the telling title "The Difference between Criticism and Hatred: Anti-American Studies." This now widely cited article characterized recent efforts to reconsider the field by such writers as Rowe, David Noble, and Donald Pease and Robin Wiegman as nothing less than revelatory of a dangerous disloyalty to the nation that gave them succor. According to Wolfe, such work represents an ominous departure from a kind of golden age of American studies, in which founders of the field including F. O. Matthiessen, Henry Nash Smith, Leo Marx, Perry Miller, and Richard Hofstadter "interpreted our culture and contemplated our character" with an appropriate appreciation of America for its "invention and energy," balanced, of course, with a healthy concern for "the excesses our way of life produced."[2] These founders were, in other words, more or less politically liberal, but also appropriately in love with America—or more specifically, in love with America as a symbol of freedom, opportunity, and futurity. Given this deep affective relationship with their object of study, these founders of the field (often remembered as the major elaborators of consensus history and American exceptionalism) would never have thought to interrogate the status, indeed the very meaning, of such phrases as "our culture" and "our civilization," to say nothing of the idea of "America" itself. By contrast, younger Americanists have come to concern themselves not only with the deep internal divisions in the history and culture of the United States, including those that take place along racial, class, ethnic, and gender lines, but with the conceptual, cultural, and political coherence and autonomy of an entity problematically called "America." If the older generations so loved America, these signs of dramatic disciplinary shift and interrogation can only signal to Wolfe the opposite of love, for both America and their elders: "The third generation and the fourth generation of scholars in the field not only reject the writers who gave life to the discipline, they have also developed a hatred for America so visceral that it makes one wonder why they bother studying America at all."[3]

Love it or leave it indeed: aren't we already familiar with the nasty business of impugning scholars' patriotism—in this case, for simply following one or another disciplinary direction? But before simply dismissing Wolfe for neo-McCarthyism (among other things; his article provides scant fodder for analysis, ultimately beating the same old anti-intellectual drums about the simultaneous triviality and disturbing power of academics), I do think it is worth pausing to consider calmly some problems Wolfe's comments may raise for us: If Americanists are busily revealing the incoherence of the symbolic "America," what is holding the habitus of the discipline together? What is our shared object? What, if anything, do we love?

To answer this question, we must return to the by now very familiar narrative of American studies' disciplinary development from consensus and exceptionalism to diversity and trans- (or even post-) nationalism. In the narrative as Wolfe would have us see it, this transition, which happened sometime around the 1960s, was characterized by a loss of faith in the meaning of America. From the perspective of the post-1960s generations of scholars, it is better characterized by a recognition of the ideological dimensions of that idea, the scholarly elaborators of which, they argued, furthered the aims of cold war politics. Much as I hate to concede anything to Wolfe, I think both of these representations of what Leo Marx has called the "Great Divide" of American studies are right: postwar American studies *was* imbued with cold war ideology, and subsequent generations *were* far more critical of the idea of America than were their elders.[4]

Nevertheless, I don't think the "Great Divide" was really so great after all. Unlike the discipline of English, which was dominated in the postwar period by an avowedly conservative (or perhaps more precisely, antipolitical) New Criticism, American studies as a field was characterized in the same period by a general Left-populist outlook, very much inherited from Depression-era cultural politics. The major figures of American studies even into the 1990s often had origins in working-class ethnic communities and were politicized in Depression-era leftist populism. But this is not to say that American studies scholars were innocent of cold war propagandizing. Frances Stonor Saunders's exhaustive study of the "cultural Cold War" offers evidence of American studies scholars' sometimes very direct participation in the anticommunist propaganda efforts of the United States. But her more general point is also salient here: much of the ideological effort directed at intellectuals in the early cold war period involved delinking their basic leftist populism from explicit sympathy for the Soviet Union. In other words, it is no contradiction that among many cold war–era scholars, nationalism, consensus, exceptionalism, and of course anticommunism could coexist with a strong and relatively continuous core of political allegiance to liberal-leftist-populist causes. In this sense, the field can be seen to generally exemplify Michael Denning's "cultural front," which formed in the Depression but which exerted a broad cultural influence well into the 1970s and 1980s.[5]

But if the "Great Divide" is overdrawn, then what is the source of this persistent narrative of pre- and post-Vietnam-era scholarship and its attendant high feelings of intergenerational rancor? The reason, I believe, that Wolfe's review has received so much attention is that it reignites some of the emotional charge of generational conflict; as in the 1960s, patricide is once again invoked as a device for dismissing the politics of the "young."[6] But also, if inadvertently, Wolfe puts his finger on what may be the more fundamental separation between pre-Vietnam-era American studies scholars and those who followed them. This generational division rests precisely in a shift in the habitus of the field regarding patriotism—or more precisely, the changing historical perceptions of the extent to which *the nation* is integral to the Left-populist political allegiances that continue to represent the core of the habitus of the field.

In the previous chapter, I discussed a basic shift in the significance of the concept of culture that occurred in the 1960s. This shift was attendant upon a larger restructuring of intellectuals' habitus toward a new interest in and solidarity with subaltern groups and movements. But this shift also entailed a basic turn away from the nation-state as the fundamental structure of social change; hence, the emergence as well in this period of supranational political movements such as environmentalism, human rights, and antineoliberalism. American studies was no less affected by this change than any other discipline in the humanities or interpretive social sciences. But what is different about American studies in this context is that it was founded on explicitly nationalist grounds, so that any shift in emphasis away from the nation (and toward, say, issues of subaltern identity) potentially represents a fundamental reconfiguration of the field's initial object of study.

Let's go back, briefly, to the 1930s, when many of the foundational works of American studies were written. In this moment, the question of nationalism was as complex as the diversity of the political positions available. The perspectives of the figures who would inspire the first generations of American studies academics are similarly difficult to characterize; they range from the Marxism of V. F. Calverton and Granville Hicks, to various kinds of idiosyncratic utopianism of figures like Lewis Mumford, to the socialism of Charles Beard and F. O. Matthiessen.[7] Nevertheless, across this spectrum their intellectual relationship to nationalism was remarkably coherent. They were, generally speaking, *cultural* nationalists, invested in the idea of a coherent American culture, different from the high cultures of Europe and connected to the popular vernacular.[8] Because it emanated from the people, this culture was also fundamentally opposed to the corruption and banality of the emergent corporate culture of the twentieth century. This was the crux also of their political vision: good populists, they fundamentally believed in the people's cultural *and political* instincts. And of course, this cultural nationalism also entailed a particular kind of patriotism, one that was almost always hostile to the interests of big business and often even at odds with the official patriotism of the U.S. government.

In the wake of World War II, the next generation of scholars who grew up reading Hicks and Mumford and who founded American studies as a discipline in the universities—the people Alan Wolfe names so approvingly—began, in the context of the cold war, to depart from the sometimes explicitly leftist politics of their predecessors. But this new generation also continued in the tradition of their predecessors in their general sympathy with the significant antisystemic movements of their moment (notably civil rights) and the general framework of cultural nationalism, which would then transmute in their hands into the more explicitly conservative forms of exceptionalism and consensus.[9] These people were also populists and patriots, but of a kind that ultimately conformed—perhaps in ways they didn't even fully appreciate—to officially promulgated conceptions of America as the torchbearer of Freedom in a riven cold war world.

So yes, the post-1960s generation of critics of the cold war ideology of American studies was generally right. But I think it is far more interesting to emphasize *their* relationship to their elders, both of the postwar period and of the generation of the 1930s Popular Front. Sympathetically attached to whole new kinds of antisystemic movements, including third-worldist Maoism, feminism, environmentalism, and black, Chicano, and gay liberation movements, the post-1960s generation revived some elements of 1930s populism—notably its persistent anticapitalist strain. But entirely uninteresting to them was the relationship of this populist habitus to nationalist feeling in any form. This may, of course, be attributed to the general climate of disillusionment of the Vietnam and Watergate years. But one must also remember in this context that the antisystemic movements to which these Americanists gave their support were uninvolved with, if not explicitly hostile to, official state nationalism.[10]

This is the fundamental ideological context of the current revisions of American studies that would tend to push it toward a more global and transnational frame, yet would nevertheless wish to do it, not in the name of American Empire, but in the postnationalist spirit of the antisystemic movements. We may now understand that it is not such a radical departure from earlier scholarship in American studies, not only in that it simply extends the now relatively long-standing critique of consensus and exceptionalism, but also in that it is full square within the habitus of the discipline. Michael Bérubé gave good evidence of this when he noted the general, if often empty, assent that scholars have given to this broad project of a postnationalist globalization of the discipline: "There is to my knowledge no such thing as a pro-imperialist American studies."[11]

YANKEE GO HOME

So at the end of the day, the sound of breaking glass may announce not a disciplinary revolution but a logical continuation of thought and habitus in the field. But what if, despite our best intentions ("There is

. . . no such thing as a pro-imperialist American studies"), the entire project of revision may somehow be complicit in contemporary ideologies of U.S. expansion? What if, perhaps like our predecessors, we are unwitting promulgators of official state ideologies? Which brings us to the "Yankee go home" problem.

In 1994, Carolyn Porter offered an important vision of a globally reconfigured American studies that "would confront (at the least) a quadruple set of relations between (1) Europe and Latin America; (2) Latin America and North America; (3) North America and Europe; and (4) Africa and both Americas."[12] Like many of the polemicists calling for a transnational American studies, Porter anticipated the ironic possibility that this well-intentioned desire to represent "America" as "internally fissured and externally relativized," might simply reflect a global scene in which America, its culture, and its political and economic systems, was now hegemonic. Indeed, one might well wonder how such a revision of the discipline would look from, say, the perspective of Latin America, where such disciplinary moves could simply be seen as the logical academic extension of sphere-of-influence politics. But interestingly, in at least one site of struggle over these proposals for revision, the cries of disciplinary "imperialism" emanated not from the South but from Europe.

Janice Radway's presidential address at the 1998 American Studies Association meeting in Seattle, which intelligently and appropriately interrogated the meaning and significance of "American studies" as a field, is now memorialized as the flashpoint for what has become hyperbolically known as "the battle of Seattle."[13] The speech (at least as published a few months after its delivery) was largely in keeping with the usual tone of retrospection and speculation about the field as a whole that the event requires, and it would have seemed strange had Radway *not* mentioned the many recent calls to redefine the field in light of recent scholarly trends. But what appears to have provoked the ire of some of her listeners (and a fair number of people reacting to secondhand reports of her talk) was the logical—but to some clearly scandalous—conclusion she drew from the trend of this work: that perhaps American studies scholars needed to rethink their problematic reliance on "America" as an organizing concept for their object of study.[14] This, she argued, not only smuggled in untenable notions of a coherent "American" identity and culture coextensive with the U.S. nation-state but linguistically replicated the nation's founding act of usurping the lands and cultures of diverse native people.

"America" as a concept, Radway insisted, contained implications of both unproblematized consensus and imperialism. Shortly after the convention, the association's e-mail list erupted with angry posts about Radway's address.[15]

Among the most prominent e-mailers were scholars of American studies working in western Europe. For them, it was not only the potential expansiveness of a field unleashed from the geographic confines implied by "America" that was imperialist but what they perceived to be an implicit call to refocus the discipline toward U.S. ethnic and racial minorities.[16] Cultural diversity, some suggested, was a problem local to the internal struggles of the United States, yet they heard Radway to be arguing for the field's reconfiguration with diversity and multiculturalism as its central preoccupation. In their view, this emphasis was then (imperialistically) imposed upon scholars working in other locales *and* on the non-American communities in which they worked. As Michael Nichols, a scholar based in Armenia, put it, "[The multiculturalism promoted by the ASA] is multiculturalism according to one dominant set of values, and the effect is to turn other cultures into pale reflections of American society. I can certainly understand when Americanists from other countries say to Radway's proposal, 'Thanks, but no thanks!'"[17]

One might paraphrase this concern as follows: The ASA is imposing a new agenda upon Americanists that is reflective of current U.S. society and its values. But these issues and values are not presented as local; they are posited as being of universal concern. Therefore, this agenda is an imperial imposition upon people elsewhere around the globe—even if it is only prescriptive for those whose scholarly work is on topics related to "America." Confusing as this argument at first seems (must the study of "America" proceed *only* from the grounds of universal values and conditions? If so, in what way would this *not* be imperialistic?), it nevertheless exemplifies some of the complexities of the "Yankee go home" problem. For Nichols's concern points to the likelihood that dissolving the idea of an internal coherency of "America" in favor of a model of complex heterogeneity can serve to mask the unstated assumption of other kinds of coherence—coherence that, furthermore, we may find problematic. Heinz Ickstadt, a former president of both the German and European American Studies Associations, put the problem this way: "As an outside observer one might argue that the study of a culture (even if it sees itself as grounded in internal difference and fragmentation) cannot be based on a study of dissent alone—as much as one cannot recognize 'otherness' without also recognizing elements of 'sameness.'"[18] The dispensing with "America" is therefore imperial-istic precisely because it allows one side of the dialectic (the side that addresses sameness, coherence, stability, and univocality) to go without saying. Not surprisingly, this problem is articulated here in disciplinary terms, so that the American Studies Association is a kind of stand-in for America, seen as positing its preoccupations as universal and imposing an agenda on those who see themselves as disciplinarily (and of course geographically) marginal.

Other battlers were even more explicit about the disciplinary impli-cations of this peculiar form of "imperialism." For David Nye, writing from Denmark, the real problem with an increased focus on multicul-turalism was institutional. Given the small size of European American studies programs, he worried that such a refocusing would entail a chan-neling of energy and personnel toward cultural diversity at the expense of attention to other kinds of diversity, especially what he saw as the central disciplinary diversity of the field.[19] An attack on the disciplinary centrality of "America" was, then, a more predictable attack on other conceptions of the core features of the field—in this case, interdiscipli-narity. In this indirect way as well, an emphasis on cultural diversity instead of a coherent "America" was a blow to the heart of the field. It is an observation that Ickstadt interestingly supports when he notes that as the coherency of the discipline has been deemphasized, American studies programs have become increasingly scarce in U.S. institutions.[20]

Indeed, we may well imagine how a challenge to the centrality of "America" might present problems for European-based Americanists, especially those housed in American studies departments and centers. Perhaps even more so than in the United States, American studies in western Europe was the product of that self-contradictory cold war–era form of exceptionalism in which America presented itself as the unique bearer to the world of the universal values of freedom and democ-racy. But if in the post–cold war era we are witnessing the spread of a global culture, and if this culture to many Europeans has a distinctly American flavor, what is the point of delineating a special area of study dedicated to "America"? How does one convince university adminis-trators to dedicate resources to departments and programs studying not a unique national culture but the hegemonic culture and political-economic system of the developed world? How does one convince U.S. governmental bodies that the propaganda value of American studies in western Europe still merits financial support? In other words, the very success of the United States after the cold war in imposing its stamp on the world has, ironically, made it less distinct (and distinctive) as an object of study. As Markku Henricksson from the University of Helsinki put it in his e-mail response to Seattle, "Will America be the world, or will the world be America?"

"CULTURE" WORRY

Henricksson, responding not to the speech but to e-mailed reports of it, glossed what he took to be Radway's gist as follows: "What I gather . . . is that Radway introduced an idea of changing the name of the American Studies Association into something where the word 'American' will be replaced by the word 'cultural.'" This characterization of Radway's speech, though ultimately unsupported by the published version, offers an opportunity to step back slightly from the local fray of one discipline to examine another, similar site of disciplinary struggle in the field of cultural anthropology. There, the scare word is not "America," of course, but "culture." But the comparison does more than bring us explicitly back to battles over the culture concept; it reveals something of the structure of disciplinary struggles in the context of globalization.

Though the words are different, these two disciplinary revisions, which focus on a central terminological node, bear strong similarities in a number of respects. As with "America" for scholars of American studies, "culture" is a term with deep communal meanings for anthropologists, especially those trained in the United States. "Culture" is often seen as connoting both the common object of study for anthropologists and the ethical stance that gives moral authority to anthropology as an enterprise. While "America" to Americanists often resonates with a generally populist allegiance to antisystemic movements, "culture" as a term similarly reverberates with the foundational belief for anthropologists in the essential value of the study of human diversity. But the similarities don't simply end with these issues of disciplinary habitus. Just as the project of interrogating the limits of "America" can be seen as deeply in keeping with the very values and principles the term also implies, the same kind of critique of "culture" emerges among anthropologists: "culture" is not, they argue, simply connotative of human diversity, it is its *negation,* serving not to highlight diversity but to delimit the practices and beliefs of Western elites. In these parallel lines of thinking, "culture" and "America" both represent sites where the habitus of fields come into conceptual conflict with those fields' objects of study. In other words, the word connoting that object of study itself—"culture" or "America"—on reflection now not only seems inadequate to the job of delineating the field but connotes obstacles to the very fulfillment of certain key features of scholars' disciplinary identities. If "America" is insufficiently reflective of the postnationalist habitus of American studies, "culture" is now often seen by anthropologists as insufficient for the full exploration of human diversity. Finally, in both cases, this crisis in the very nature of the object of study is expressed in terms of fear of potential disciplinary loss—on the one hand of the coherence of the discipline in the form of a discrete object of study, on the other hand of the discipline itself to other disciplinary interlopers. The likely interloper also represents a point of convergence, in that for many anthropologists, and indeed Americanists like Henricksson, it is clearly cultural studies.

But I will go even further and press the similarity in these two revisions into a kind of chiasmic pattern. The similarity between these two sites leads me to believe that a central, if largely unspoken problem with "culture" for many anthropologists is its associations with nationalism. Conversely, we might conclude that one of the problems with "America" may very well be its *culturalism,* that is, its tendency to be irreducible to one national culture but to require an attention to its diversity. From this point forward, I will address the anthropological critique of culture in connection with the critique of "America," for finally, I see them as of a piece: both are intimately connected to the academic response to globalization.

One of the truly time-honored ways in which the idea of "culture" has been used has been to separate out one group of people and their practices from another. "Culture," as Fredric Jameson has remarked, is "an idea of the Other (even when I reassume it for myself)."[21] In this sense, discussions of disciplinarity—which are often about whole dispositions of behavior, belief, morality, the works—neatly replicate, structurally, the logic of an important strain of cultural analysis. Similarly, calls to interrogate the status of our theoretical assumptions are not simply about theory; they are also exercises in imagining the community of interlocutors and the behavior that defines them as distinct. These moments of self-conscious disciplinary formation and definition are also sites of what might easily be termed *cultural* production and maintenance. In other words, though "culture" sometimes seems inadequate to describing the complexity of human behavior, it often does the job rather well of describing how we sometimes operate. In other words, it is not the *term* that people want to get beyond (if that were even possible), but certain kinds of sites of bounded group formation that the term has been used to describe. Hence, my suggestion that what may be particularly haunting the concept of culture is its close relationship to constructions of nationalism.

As I have already noted, one of the main functions of the Boasian culture concept was to disrupt a central assumption of romantic nationalism: that the nation politically confirmed the unity of a people who were already triply united by a common language, folk culture, and race or "blood." Yet I think that for many of "culture's" critics this delinking of culture from nationalism is still only rudimentary. Structurally, "culture" still seems to recapitulate the largely static and undynamic spatial model that is at the core of most conceptions of the nation-state. Thus "culture" often connotes a kind of ideological horizon that determines who gets included within the nation and who gets excluded from it. For example, much of the symbolic politics of the "culture wars" in the United States seems based, on all sides, on the implicit premise that if you have a recognized place in the official records and canons of American culture, then you also have a legitimate place in the nation-state and its apparatuses of power and prestige. Then too, various racial or ethnic essentialisms have been described as operating like nation-states, in the sense that they posit static constructions of identity and firmly patrolled borders of inclusion and exclusion. My provisional hypothesis, therefore, is that the desire to get beyond culture may instead be a desire to get beyond, by another name, this conception of the nation and its attendant nationalist fantasy of coherence and cohesion. The desire to get beyond nationalism, in turn, is symptomatic of a much larger shift in the conceptualization of social space. This reconceptualization involves a response not only to nationalism and the subnationalisms of various kinds of group identity but to globalization itself, which at times seems to promise some kind of wholesale transcendence of the fixities of the nation-state.

AMERICAN/CULTURE

Though it should by now go without saying, I do not see much point in either changing the name of American studies or getting beyond "culture." In fact, given the considerable popular rhetoric surrounding these terms, I think it would be a terrible idea for academics to cede the rhetorical field on these particular sites. Rather, what I am calling for is precisely the opposite gesture: a vigorous intensification of our rhetorical analysis of both crucial sites, resulting in a conscious and strategic deployment of both "America" and "culture," in the context of our current geopolitical realities.

"America" has a special status with regard to the topic of globalization, a status, moreover, that is still a matter of intense discussion. Asserting that "Imperialism is over" and that "no nation will be world leader in the way modern European nations were," Michael Hardt and Antonio Negri remind us that the United States is not, in any simple way, the latest, and most total, replacement for the great nineteenth-century imperial powers.[22] Which is not, however, to say that the United States is in any way marginal to a new regime they call "Empire." As David Harvey reminds us, the current moment of accelerated globalization is "the outcome of a geopolitical crusade waged largely by the United States" in the wake of World War II.[23] To move "beyond" nationalist schemas to global frames in a way that ignores this history could thus be seen as an attempt to repackage agendas still very closely connected with U.S. national policy in a new form. Which is to say that without some serious thought concerning these new spatial and conceptual challenges, American studies could become again what it was accused of being in its early days by the post-1960s revisionists: a propaganda wing for the global ambitions of U.S. corporate and political power. Put another way, we may want to consider the polemical and theoretical possibilities in reviving Antonio Gramsci's concept of "Americanism," a term of an earlier period that, if we were to explore it, seems to me to have the advantage of complexly foregrounding the issue of political and cultural agency.[24]

For indeed, globalization is not just a set of adjustments in the regulation and flows of people and capital. It is also a rhetoric and an ideology, as anyone familiar with the popular business and management literature of the moment can attest.[25] One feature of this rhetoric is to insist on a certain relation to historicity. Like the rhetoric of consumer culture, that of globalization tends to suggest both imminent futurity and the dramatic obsolescence of previous structures and ways of being, a kind of revving up of the old narrative of modernity's dissolution into air of all that had once seemed so solid. In this rush for the new, it may therefore be the survivors and remnants of old ways of being and thinking, what Evan Watkins has called the "throwaways," that will then serve as sites of alterity, opposition, and possibility.[26] It has long been noted that nationalism persists as a key political force in postcolonial contexts and may still have an important role to play in the resistance to certain new forms of imperialism that come under the name of globalization. So are we now, in our global moment, in a position where, ironically, the nation can be seen as such a holdover and can therefore serve this kind of function?

A common view of nationalism is that it tends to divide people up along national lines, according to what Freud called the "narcissism of minor differences."[27] But I think Wallerstein is right to remind us that nationalism is not just a force of particularity; it has also been a powerful force of homogenization. Structurally, nation-states today are all similar to each other in a number of basic respects: they all have legislatures, currencies, militaries, school systems, national anthems, a state-sponsored folk culture, a state-sponsored high culture, state-sponsored historical monuments, and so forth.[28] So even as nationalism has encouraged an elaboration of differences, it has simultaneously promoted a structural similarity *among* nations, in which nation-states are the norm and, conversely, to be a "stateless person" is an anomalous, and rather terrible, situation to be in.

The same point can be made of globalization, if in reverse. Even among some of its most ardent champions, it is perceived as a notoriously homogenizing force, threatening to supplant local specificity and control with what is usually despaired of as a mediocre sameness.[29] This, for example, seems to be at least one of the stock messages behind the extensive press coverage of the installation of a Starbucks coffee shop in Vienna, across from the city's famed opera house: corporate blueberry muffins and mochachinos have at last supplanted centuries of Viennese coffeehouse culture.[30] But in other domains, it is clear that globalization does not produce homogenization at all but rather has intensified the production of new particularities, whole new polyglot forms of exotica, of people, objects, and ideas recombining in new ways and places. Against the alleged obliteration of local color represented by the image of Starbucks in Vienna, we might as easily invoke, say, the popularity of Bollywood films in West Africa, or the adoption, in France, of parts of hip-hop culture by the children of Algerian immigrants.[31] In the United States, university students joined with Mexican and Central American migrant workers to protest seasonal farm labor conditions by boycotting Taco Bell, a major purchaser of the tomatoes and onions picked by these laborers and a major purveyor of vaguely Mexican-inspired fast food on and around university campuses. (The protesters' clever slogan, spoofing Taco Bell's advertising, was "Yo no quiero Taco Bell.")[32] This is but one example of the way that the forces of globalization have also helped produce particularities in reaction and protest.

But it is important to emphasize that what is effective and significant about such protests is that they are *protests,* and not that they are particularities. That is, nothing about particularity is inherently opposed to globalization's homogenizing tendencies. Rather, this great homogenizing juggernaut of global capital may well *need* particularity. Out of particularity comes exploitable populations of workers. The resurgence of the sweatshop and piecework in the United States is due not only to the sad state of the American labor movement but to the existence of highly mobile populations of workers from around the world who wind up working where they do because of their particular place in a mesh of specific social, cultural, linguistic, and legal contexts. For example, in Silicon Valley, multinational corporations outsource the assembly of high-tech goods to entrepreneurial immigrant subcontractors, who in turn employ mostly female workers of their own nationality and ethnic group to do the piecework assembly at extremely depressed rates of pay. They are able to do this in part because of bonds of obligation, custom, and fear of retaliation within the immigrant communities.[33] Also, it is out of various particularities that we get the novelty that drives consumerism: new sites for the production and consumption of new kinds of goods, images, information, needs, and desires. It is often noted that these new sites of particularity are susceptible to becoming homogenized all over again through the processes of commodification. While this speaks to the close relationship of the cultural and the economic in the current moment, I don't think it changes my point materially, that the production of particularities is integral to globalization.

There is, of course, nothing new about this process. Corporations, and before them capitalists of other sorts, have sought new markets and products and exploited the cheap labor of mobile populations for a long time now. Moreover, I would argue that the larger dynamic is also nothing new but is in fact a constitutive feature of modernity, whose upheavals and dislocations have always created new forms of both homogenization and particularity. For example, it is one of the central contradictions of capitalism that for their labor to be exploited workers must be "freed" from traditional economies, but for capitalists to control the labor market barriers must also be placed to workers' mobility. While the former pressure tends to consolidate diverse peoples into a mass of laborers, the latter tends to turn the mobile mass once again into locally dispersed peoples. It has been persuasively suggested that in Africa this dynamic of creating alternately mobile and rooted populations is at the heart of much of the current intergroup violence that erupts around various claims to autochthony.[34] In other words, despite the dizzying rhetoric of falling borders and accelerating flows of people and goods, the experience of globalization may be characterized less as an intensification of homogenization than as an intensification of *both* homogenization *and* the production of new particularities. Which is to say, globalization is nothing more (or less) than an intensification of capitalism.

At this point we can say the following about "culture" in this changing spatio-temporal context: if culture is the site of the production of particularities, and those particularities themselves are not necessarily sites of resistance to globalization (but rather complexly, dialectically, intrinsic to it), then culture is also not necessarily a site of resistance. Now, this conclusion could lead to a kind of political despair in that it underscores the difficulty of actually theorizing and even locating resistance in the current context. For example, it prevents one from seeing resistance in every alternative cultural practice, subculture, or space of difference—a move that was common a while back in some versions of cultural studies. On the other hand, I believe it shows us how culture can continue to operate as an important analytic term in the context of globalization, for in this moment, to talk about "culture" in all its complexity is in fact to talk about one of the central dynamics of globalization itself, the production of particularities in and through and sometimes also against the production of homogeneity and totality. This, I believe, is the substance of what Hardt and Negri mean when they argue that "what needs to be addressed . . . is precisely the production of locality, that is, the social machines that create and recreate the identities and differences that are understood as the local."[35] Hence talking about "culture" in this moment could, should, be much more than simply talking in coded ways about the nation-state (and/or its apparent irrelevance). It could actually help us find a way to connect the various complex layers of analysis that this present situation requires.

One of the more pernicious features of the ideology of the homogenization of culture under globalization—the spread of U.S.-originating brand names such as Starbucks, McDonalds, and Coca-Cola to the detriment of local business, health, and ambience—is the way that it serves as a naturalization of the real homogenizing forces of our current moment. For what are really being structured worldwide are not the diversity of local choices in coffee and sodas but the larger apparatuses that directly impinge on the flow of capital. Legal codes governing the transfer of people, things, and ideas across borders are being made more uniform internationally, while local relations and regulations of labor and capital are being actively displaced in the service of ever freer free markets. This, obviously, is a root cause behind the ever-widening gap, globally, between the haves and the have-nots. What we should be paying attention to, in other words, is not the depressing predictability and charmlessness of corporate fast food but the economic forces that allow the global penetration of these companies: neoliberalism, or what Naomi Klein has aptly called the "happy meal" of McGovernment.[36] An attention, in other words, to the complex cultural dynamics of globalization may at least help us to disentangle the processes of innovation and exchange from the political, economic, and ideological frameworks that currently guide how homogeneity and particularity are globally dispersed.

What, then, are the lessons here for American studies in the context of globalization? The first, I think, is to recognize that an American studies should now proceed from a complex understanding of the global totality, even as we develop a nuanced conception of the United States as both an ideological figuration and a discrete entity. That is, we may need to suspend our well-practiced aversion to exceptionalism long enough to address the United States as its own particularity, existing and changing in specific and ungeneralizable ways—even as we recognize that it is complexly related to other localities both internal and external to its borders. Indeed, we need to think very carefully about the specificity of America and its history in this moment most of all; for if the United States is a driving engine of neoliberalism then we need to historicize its particular development in order to denaturalize it as the only system under which we may now live. We thus also need to apply the temporal axis of cultural analysis to considerations of "America." For, when followed through, the study of cultural change reveals not only the unpredictability of cultural creativity, contact, and conflict but the possibility of the unexpected. This is the axis of hope; the site of culture's—and "America's"—meaning as a space of struggle and possibility. No sound of shattering glass accompanies this suggestion; like the proposals of many disciplinary revisionists, it too is fully in keeping with the habitus of the field.

CHAPTER 5

The Santa Claus Problem

Culture, Belief, Modernity

CULTURE IS BANAL

A few years ago, a friend showed me an advertisement from the pages of the *Economist* whose prominent slogan had caught her notice: "Never underestimate the importance of local knowledge." The slogan was illustrated with three pictures of different kinds of sweets: a tray of Belgian spekulaas cookies, a plate of British mince pies, and a bowl of Swedish rice pudding. My friend, a recent BA in anthropology, at the time had the job market very much on her mind and so took it as a sign that former anthropology majors, academically trained to worry about "local knowledge," had for good or ill infiltrated Madison Avenue. I on the other hand, read it as yet another sign of the basic banality of much contemporary discourse and understanding of culture. Here, knowledge of local culture—in this case, knowledge of which festive Christmas treat is served in which northern European country—apparently keeps HSBC, which brands itself "The World's Local Bank," from being just another global corporation with offices in seventy-nine countries and territories. As the ad copy says, "Being local enables [HSBC] to offer insights into financial opportunities and create service initiatives that would never occur to an outsider." So knowledge of local culture is, on the one hand, what is asserted to make all the difference in the context of something we might hesitantly denominate global corporate culture. On the other hand, it seems to come down to the rather trivial matter of one's Christmas dessert menu—which is to say that cultural difference (already somewhat shallowly conceived) is nothing much more serious than a set of innocuous consumer choices.

This sense of triviality is only heightened by the fact that at about the same time as HSBC was running its festive ad, the major news outlets were covering a series of deadly terrorist bombings in Istanbul that had targeted several synagogues, the British consulate, and HSBC's fifteen-story Istanbul branch.[1] Juxtaposed with the plates of sweets, this dramatic event certainly seemed to put into question HSBC's confident assertions about the fluency or efficacy of its local knowledge. But some might go further. To some, this suicide bombing—the ultimate expression of commitment to some cause—serves as the kind of gesture that gives lie to the pretensions of cultural discourse as a whole. What do cultural differences matter in a world where suicide bombers can exist? Which is to say more precisely: What do knowledge and tolerance of other cultures matter, when others hold (by definition repugnant) views for which they are willing to both kill and die? Certainly, this line of thinking might conclude, the central issue now for students of humanity is not the endless elaboration of cultural difference but rather unraveling the mystery of the suicide bomber: the difference with potentially fatal consequences, the mystery of *belief*.

In other words, in precisely the moment when the idea of culture seems played out, religion has returned as a hot topic. Thus we have seen a resurgence in interest in religion in some likely and unlikely places. In addition to Charles Taylor's magisterial recent history of secularism, there has been a notable critical engagement with religion—especially Christianity—among European Marxists and leftists including Giorgio Agamben, Alain Badiou, Jean-Luc Nancy, and Slavoj Žižek.[2] We must also note in this context the proliferation of antireligious tracts by the likes of Richard Dawkins, Sam Harris, and Christopher Hitchens.[3] While the specter of the suicide bomber— of extreme religious fundamentalism—hovers around these new religious conversations, there are other phenomena and contexts at work here as well. While the vast migrations and social upheavals of recent decades have contributed to the worldwide explosion in Pentecostal and Charismatic Christianity, Jean and John Comaroff point out the recent global proliferation of "occult economies" of witchcraft, divination, zombies, pyramid schemes, and conspiracy theories: new organizations of belief that have grown up in the shadow of neoliberalism.[4]

FROM CULTURE TO BELIEF

Very shortly after 9/11, it became a disturbing truism among conservative pundits that in some ways the tragedy of that day was a good thing. 9/11 had apparently caused a dramatic change in the zeitgeist, so that suddenly (according to James Pinkerton) "irony, cynicism, and hipness" were unfashionable, to be replaced, even in "trendoid" New York, by "sincerity, patriotism, and earnestness"—and "a lot of spontaneous non-sexual hugging and kissing."[5] Postmodern irony and playfulness—and sex—had apparently made way for a new gravitas of soul-searching and a return to core values. And in some ways, a new academic attention to globalization fit right in with the mood of the moment, not only bringing into focus the geopolitical context of the terrorist attacks of that day but also, it seemed, dealing with the kind of "serious" questions heretofore relegated to such quantitative social scientific fields as political science and economics (and to a lesser extent geography). It also, as I have already mentioned, promised the end of the postmodern ban on a number of analytic categories more or less associated with the Marxist tradition: capitalism, modernity, totality. In this context, it is no surprise that the "culture" of the cultural turn, with its emphasis on agency and the multifarious improvisations of discrete human actors, and its status as a product of interpretive disciplines, seemed outmoded, even trivial. For these fields, "seriousness" would often be sought in a new turn to ethics and to questions of religion and religious belief.

But even before 2001, belief of a kind was making its comeback—in a more or less culturalist guise. Samuel Huntington's notorious "clash of civilizations" hypothesis, which posited a new alignment of ideological struggle for the post–cold war world, was first and foremost a reply to an earlier and equally controversial post–cold war polemic, Francis Fukuyama's "End of History" thesis, which asserted that the unopposed triumph of political and economic liberalism marked the end of ideological struggle altogether.[6] For Huntington, on the other hand, ideological struggle would simply shift to another axis: one based in ethnic identity (the culturalist part of his argument) but grounded in the doctrinal differences of religion. Indeed, for Huntington, the line that once divided NATO and Warsaw Pact countries is simply revealed to be the old border between the regions dominated by Roman Catholicism and Protestantism ("Western Christianity") on the one hand, and Orthodox Christianity and Islam on the other: "The velvet curtain of culture has replaced the iron curtain of ideology as the most significant dividing line in Europe."[7]

The culturo-religious context of Huntington's argument is also evident in his otherwise somewhat incoherent list of global "civilizations": Western, Confucian, Japanese, Islamic, Hindu, Slavic-Orthodox, Latin American, and *"possibly* African civilization."[8] At least, the category of religious difference helps to makes sense of his denominations of "Confucian," "Islamic," "Hindu," and "Slavic-Orthodox" civilizations. As for the Western, Japanese, Latin American, and African civilizations, where religion is less clearly the central organizational principle, one can only guess that the rationale for these categories is both simplification (how does one denominate *the* religion of Africa or Japan?) and heightened incommensurability: Latin America shares Roman Catholicism with much of Europe and North America, yet remains for Huntington profoundly *other*.[9] But the real odd civilization out is not Latin America or Japan, or even the apparently dubious African civilization, but the West. For the West is ultimately characterized for Huntington by a distinctive postreligious position: that of Enlightenment secular humanism.

In this respect, the West occupies for Huntington a position in every way analogous to that given to America by cold war ideologues who held the United States to be simultaneously (and contradictorily) the universal ideal to which all aspired and a historically unique cradle of freedom. Now the West (which in Huntington's work easily transposes into the United States) is both the unique bearer to the world of secular humanism, a specific historical invention, and the universal position that trumps all others. Huntington quotes V. S. Naipaul to argue that "Western civilization is the 'universal civilization' that 'fits all men.'" But he simultaneously notes that in the new moment of civilizational clash such universalism nevertheless encounters "cultural" resistance: "Western ideas of individualism, liberalism, constitutionalism, human rights, equality, liberty, the rule of law, democracy, free markets, the separation of church and state, often have little resonance in Islamic, Confucian, Japanese, Hindu, Buddhist or Orthodox cultures."[10] In other words, the West must be locatable as the embattled province of a specific set of global actors and represent a kind of natural state to which everyone aspires—or at least would aspire if freed from the shackles of their particularizing religion-cultures.[11]

It would be tempting to say that Huntington's secular humanism is itself a kind of religion, in the sense that William James observed a century ago among his contemporaries: "Any 'habitual and regulated admiration,' says Professor J.R. Seeley, 'is worthy to be called a religion'; and accordingly, he thinks that our Music, our Science, and our so-called 'Civilization,' as these things are now organized and admiringly believed in, form the more genuine religions of our time. Certainly the unhesitating and unreasoning way in which we feel that we must inflict our civilization upon 'lower' races, by means of Hotchkiss guns, etc., reminds one of nothing so much as of the early spirit of Islam spreading its religion by the sword."[12] But for James, a general sense of admiration, either alone or combined with missionary zeal, wasn't enough to add up to religious feeling, and the same might be said of many of Huntington's fellow admirers of Western civilization. For apparently, and perhaps more dramatically than with its cold war analogue, liberal humanism doesn't seem to provide either the affect or the sense of identity associated with religious faith. In short, liberal humanism doesn't feel like much of a belief at all.

Take, for example, the cartoon controversy of 2006, in which a Danish newspaper editor invited cartoonists to submit images of Muhammad. The ensuing death threats and demonstrations attendant on the publication of the blasphemous images were frequently posed in the European and American press as examples of the intolerance of the fanatical Islamic world, as opposed to the values of the secular humanist West. But for at least a few commentators, the asymmetry between the West and the rest was rather one of belief. Thus, for Stanley Fish, the clear religious principles of the offended Muslims were met with what Fish controversially (and perhaps unfortunately) described as "the religion of letting it all hang out": a liberal faith in nothing more than a vague and largely inconsequential respect for others' rights to self-expression—not only irrespective of content, but even when the content of that expression contradicted the tenets of liberalism itself.[13]

Predictably, plenty of bloggers and editorial writers replied to Fish by filling in the specifics of a credo for liberalism; they cited individualism, human rights, equality, liberty, the rule of law, democracy, the separation of church and state, and so forth. In other words, they sounded rather like Huntington in his description of a postreligious West. For indeed, rather than being tenets of some kind of political faith, these ideas are instead the juridical cornerstones of the Western defense *against* the abusive exercise of beliefs in the political arena. In other words, as much as one may passionately believe in human rights or the rule of law, the centrality of these concepts tends to confirm Fish's point that what we believe in most fervently is freedom from having others' beliefs imposed upon us (or anyone else). That is to say, what liberalism believes in, according to Fish, is precisely freedom from belief: if there is a liberal humanist subject position, it is one constituted around a fundamentally negative principle.[14]

A few respondents to Fish seemed to intuit this negativity, if only to impute to Fish an identity crisis in the form of a secret wish to be more like the Muslim protesters. Just as George Orwell once explained away British communism in the 1930s as the "patriotism of the deracinated," these writers portrayed Fish as an unmoored postmodernist longing for the solidity of belief in whatever form.[15] Fish's other writings suggest a different view: that the real issue is rather his distaste for positions like liberal humanism that hold themselves up as easy and platitudinous universals.[16] The Muslim protesters, in other words, serve as reminders for Fish both that all beliefs—including liberalism's belief in political freedom from being constrained by the beliefs of others—are contextual and situational and that this in no way lessens the power they have for the people who hold them. In a sense, then, Fish used the issue of belief to expose the contradiction at the heart of contemporary ideologies of Western humanism, which claims universality on the grounds that it somehow transcends belief, and therefore succumbs to both raw ideology and severe internal contradiction. Examples such as the Danish cartoon incident reveal that liberalism cracks under the pressure of trying to tolerate those who do not tolerate liberalism itself. For indeed, these intolerant others simply reveal liberalism to be one set of beliefs among others.

Another way of saying this, of course, is that all beliefs emanate from a cultural context. And yet such a basic pronouncement is also liable to provoke. Returning to the issue of banality with which this chapter started, Slavoj Žižek argues that in the West "culture" is not the intimate context of belief but rather its opposite: the ritual stuff that we do *without belief,* like paying homage to Santa Claus at Christmas time. According to him, we exist in something like a cultural version of Weber's religious "iron cage." Just as for Weber religion once gave meaning to capitalist enterprise until it fell a victim of modernity's rationalizations, leaving only hollow forms of behavior, so now for Žižek does culture somehow contain or compel our behavior, even though we don't need to believe that our culture is in any way vital to us, our well-being, even our identity. "'Culture' is the name for all those things we practice without really believing in them, without 'taking them seriously.'"[17]

But importantly for Žižek, there are still others who have not achieved this level of compartmentalization: "And is this . . . not why we dismiss fundamentalist believers as 'barbarians,' as anticultural, as a threat to culture—they dare to *take their beliefs seriously?*"[18] To make this point Žižek offers us the challenging example of the Taliban, who dynamited the giant Buddha statues in Bamiyan—an act that many observers quite reasonably termed cultural vandalism. Žižek argues that what the Taliban confronts and appalls us with in this act is the very fervor of their belief, which therefore admits of no other possibilities. So while the rest of the world looked on in horror over the destruction of what the German minister of culture called a part of the "global cultural heritage," the Taliban saw nothing but the eradication of idols, of what the Mullah Omar called an "affront to Islam."[19]

But perhaps there is some terminological confusion here—again, circulating around "culture." For in Žižek's sense, and that of those who use phrases like "global cultural heritage," culture is precisely a part of the liberal universalism that Fish described as essentially vacuous: a category of objects whose value and significance are by definition universally accepted, yet which requires no strong allegiance from us. Indeed, as with the Danish cartoons, the issue surrounding the Buddhas often seems to be not about content but about an abstract principle. For it seems clear that those who denounced the Taliban's act of destruction were on the whole far less concerned with the statues themselves—as figures with intrinsic religious, historical, aesthetic, or even personal significance—than they were with the categorical view that things that are impressive in some way (old, big, beautiful, etc.) ought not to be blown up.

So in this sense, Žižek's complaint about what we might call Santa Claus culture is in line with Fish's concerns about what he called "liberalism": both represent a fundamentally flawed projection of a Western universalism that, among other things, leaves us baffled at the behavior of those who feel, sometimes rather passionately, otherwise. Nor is this an inconsequential matter, for this sense of bafflement and outrage extends well beyond the Danish cartoon protests and the destruction in Bamiyan to such globally transformative events as the 1979 Iranian revolution and the puzzlement that continues to be expressed in many quarters over why the Iraqi people don't seem to be happy about U.S. occupation ("Why do they hate us?").[20]

But there is another component of this implicit opposition—"our" universal culture versus "their" barbarian beliefs—that still needs to be explored. For in this formulation there is also a strong compensatory fantasy at work. I would argue that from this position of Western universality we also imagine, indeed *wish*, that others—even the Taliban—are under the sway of powerful beliefs. Žižek cites a common misperception in the early anthropological literature on religion that held that "primitive" peoples believed in some profoundly different way than modern subjects in such ritual matters as totemism or witchcraft—believed, say, that their clan literally descended from a fish, or believed in the consistent efficacy of magical rites.[21] This, of course, is another example of romantic othering that assumes that there are "primitives" and that they think and behave in a fundamentally incommensurate fashion. In fact, history has shown that when the magic doesn't work, or Jesus or the UFOs don't appear at the prophesied hour, people all over do pretty much the same thing: they come up with an explanation in keeping with their belief system that fully accounts for what is now regarded as an anomaly.[22] But as an example of romantic othering, this view that the primitive has some special form of real belief also contains a kernel of desire: a wish that one could also believe, as perhaps a child does, in the magic of Santa Claus. (Or, more precisely, a *young* child: one not yet in that state of half-belief that also entails a covering of one's bets).

But this desire extends beyond a kind of wishful projection of naïveté onto the other. It also exists in the widely held and equally romantic view that tribal or so-called primitive people somehow exist in an unmediated and unalienated relationship to "their culture." These imaginary others are therefore necessarily concerned to preserve "their culture" from the onslaughts of market capitalism, environmental degradation, religious conversion, and so forth. They not only want to, but indeed must by their very makeup, remain authentic. Correspondingly, in this cultural fantasy, our Western lack of belief also works to our Western advantage, in that unlike those imagined tribal people we are not bound to our culture and are able to move between and across cultural sites, like good tourists of religious exotica, stopping one week in Bamiyan, another week in Mecca or Goa or Dharamsala. Moreover, not only are these romantic primitives incapable of saying, "I don't really believe in this; it's just part of my culture," they are in some sense incapable of speaking of their culture at all, for to do so would already imply that culture's reification and the speaker's alienation from it. In other words, the primitive has authentic culture (which we may also call belief), while the West has the discourse of culture. In this sense, both belief and culture are asymmetrically allocated in our world, with what Žižek denominates as the West possessing a good degree of mobile culture, and the rest bearing for us the burden of belief.

Returning briefly to the HSBC ad, this same logic also helps explain why we must apparently pay attention to the matter of Christmas treats: not because we find the difference between rice pudding, mince pies, and spekulaas to be very important but because we earnestly believe that other people—Swedish, British, and Belgian—do. A helpful little pamphlet called *Business Connections: Your Guide to Business Culture around the World*, which HSBC made available for download from their corporate website, clarifies the real meaning and significance of global cultural differences.[23] There we learn about the importance in China of developing "guanxi," or close personal relationships, and we are told not to exhibit signs of impatience in the United Arab Emirates. We are reminded that when we are in Brazil we mustn't try to conduct business in Spanish, while we are prepped to expect "passionate" business encounters in France. But beyond these facile pointers, the central message is that culture counts precisely because *other* people are likely to be constrained by theirs—while a savvy international businessperson remains unconstrained; once he or she is armed with a (very) few basic points of etiquette and common sense ("local knowledge" amounts to nothing much more difficult than remembering that they speak Portuguese in Brazil), cultural differences are rendered insignificant.

In this regard, it is relevant to note that HSBC, which now boasts operations in eighty-two countries and territories, began its history in 1865 as the Hong Kong and Shanghai Banking Corporation, a venerable financial arm of the British Empire.[24] For indeed, there is an old trope of imperialist literature that imagines precisely the kind of asymmetrical cultural movement embodied in HSBC's publicity. Think only of Rudyard Kipling's Kim, who is capable of moving about India in a variety of disguises—as a Hindu, a Muslim, a Christian, and so forth. Not only does Kim's capacity for cultural passing go largely undetected, but it is a knack that is peculiarly his, inaccessible to the native Indians he encounters. The natives are stuck in their culture (again, defined via their religion), but the protean boy of mixed European and Indian ancestry is not. Or, to take an American example, we might think of the long tradition in this country of "playing Indian"—that is, of ethnic Europeans adopting what they see as authentic American Indian clothes, customs, and so forth. While white people in America apparently have this unique ability to step into, and then just as importantly out of, the cultures of the people whom they have conquered, when Indians adopt European manners, it's called assimilation.[25] In other words, it's seen as a loss of one culture in accommodation to another. Or worse, when the "native" person steps into the context of the imperial culture, it can be seen as an act of terrible effrontery and even violence. The Taliban's destruction of the Buddhas was all the more horrifying in the Western imagination precisely because they were destroying objects of "*global cultural heritage.*" Compare this level of outrage to the Taliban's treatment of Afghani women, whose plight—that is, until 9/11—was too often dismissed as a lamentable feature of the local culture.[26]

CULTURE AND BELIEF

So we see that culture and belief are often distributed asymmetrically, where a mobile, mutable, self-referential culture (and its discourse) are allocated to "the West," while an authentic culture-as-belief is allocated to the other. The kind of culture that is often attributed to the "enlightened" West is both powerful, in that it is to be universally admired and emulated, and felt to be hollow at its core, the product of modern alienation and rationalization. The West's plight is anomie and alienation (culture without belief); for the rest, the problem is that they are supposed to aspire to just such a state. This, of course, is the sense in which the discourse of culture has become imbricated with the fatal ideology of modernity.

There are good and obvious reasons why this kind of position, with its central tropes of primitivism and Orientalism, has been so thoroughly interrogated and undone. For some, undoing this self-contradictory assemblage necessarily entails getting rid of culture too.[27] But is the problem here with culture or with this lopsided narrative of modernity, which seems to have made such a roaring comeback in the face of the United States' global war on terror? I will propose that it is this narrative of modernity—but not modernity itself—that requires dismantling. But to dismantle it, we must clarify culture's relationship to modernity.

"All of a sudden," reports Marshall Sahlins, "everyone got 'culture.' Australian Aboriginals, Inuit, Easter Islanders, Chambri, Ainu, Bushmen, Kayapo, Tibetans, Ojibway: even peoples whose ways of life were left for dead or dying a few decades ago now demand an indigenous space in a modernizing world under the banner of their 'culture.' They use that very word, or some near local equivalent."[28] If Sahlins is right—and I think he is—then we may see this acquisition of culture as a relatively recent historical event. That alone seems to confirm the common narrative that the appropriation of the idea of culture by non-Western people is a sign of their modernization. Indeed, it has often been suggested that the idea of culture is nothing more than part of the imperial project of sorting peoples into administrative units and that the adoption of the language of culture by non-Western peoples, in turn, represents nothing more than their acquiescence to Western conceptual schemas.[29] From this vantage, it is hard not to see the adoption of self-referential cultural identities as part of a process of raw commodification in which indigenous knowledge, arts traditions, symbols, sacred sites, spiritual practices, and even whole "cultures" are being redefined as forms of alienable property.[30] Or, if cultures are not literally becoming property, then their reification entails other kinds of circulation—in, for example, political discourse—in ways that don't necessarily serve the needs and interests of indigenous people.[31]

On the other hand, there are a number of well-known cases in which "getting 'culture'" has been seen in specific contexts to have some clear benefits, not least being participation within a global political economic system. As Terence Turner showed in a well-known essay, acquiring a sense of the possession of a distinctive culture—in part through contact with outsiders with ethnological interests—allowed the Kayapo of the southern Amazon to articulate a new sense of themselves as social actors within the wider frame of Brazilian and even international contexts. Whereas, according to Turner, the Kayapo were in the 1960s beset by the combined miseries of the corrupt and neglectful Brazilian government, missionization, and environmental destruction, the recognition and self-promotion of their distinctive cultural identity gave the Kayapo a new and powerful bargaining chip, bringing a powerful set of international players to aid them in their heretofore regional struggles: ethnographers, aid workers, environmentalists, media personalities, and others, whose largely first-world resources could be mobilized on the Kayapo's behalf. This may all be understood cynically, as a story not only of inauthenticity and alienation but of bald manipulation (Turner himself compares it to the way that third-world leaders played off the superpowers during the cold war). But the effects of the Kayapo "resurgence" seem undeniable: in the period of the 1970s and 1980s, under the sway of the idea of a distinctive cultural identity, the Kayapo successfully took control of the institutions that mediate between the

Kayapo and the larger Brazilian society and waged a series of impressively successful political campaigns for indigenous rights, environmental protection, and land use, and against the political intimidation of their leaders.[32]

In some ways, the question of whether one tends to see such stories as ones of loss or triumph is related to a philosophical problem deeply embedded in the Marxist philosophical tradition. While some would hold that alienation is solely the consequence of human labor's entry into capitalism (implying that there is some other or prior state of unalienated labor), others would contend that alienation—or better, externalization *(Entäusserung)*—is part of the general human condition: a self-consciousness about one's existence. In the former sense, any entry into the terms of global capitalism is a disaster; in the latter sense, the acquisition of culture is nothing more (or less) than the human act of self-understanding—that is, philosophy itself.[33]

The political, economic, and historical implications of this kind of externalization are necessarily multivalent in ways that make the best sense out of situations such as that facing the Kayapo. While their apparently recent acquisition of a self-conscious conception of culture lays the groundwork for various new kinds of exploitation—and for the rigidification of ideas of Kayapo culture so especially deplored by anthropologists—it is also a precondition for their new-found political empowerment, which has taken on characteristics that seem by turns capitalist and anticapitalist, Euro-Brazilian and Kayapo. But if this kind of cultural self-consciousness creates multivalently good and bad effects, I think it is also true that the political empowerment that has enabled their resurgence requires some degree of externalization. As Sahlins notes, a self-reflexive understanding of culture not only preserves the idea of cultural difference but carves out a space for critique as well. Those who claim possession of a specific culture "back their claims with references to distinctive traditions and customs that typically involve invidious contrast to the money-love and other character defects of their erstwhile colonial masters. 'If we didn't have *kastom*,' the New Guinean said to his anthropologist, 'we would be just like White Men.'"[34] In this respect, a reflexive conception of one's culture presents a context for estranging not only one's own values but those of the West as well.

So what does all this entail for belief? I have already portrayed belief and culture as starkly different from each other: while culture is a realm of difference associated with the past and the passing of the old ways, belief seems to represent alterity fully and intractably existing in the present. Indeed, belief may well be what we call that which is resistant to this kind of process of reification that seems to bedevil culture. In other words, belief remains worrisome in a way that these narratives of culture expressly do not, precisely because it appears to present a challenge to another central tenet of the ideology of modernity, namely its universal applicability. This is one of the senses behind such statements as that by Richard Dawkins that religious belief is "nothing less than a global assault on rationality, and the Enlightenment values that inspired the founding of this first and greatest of secular republics."[35] Which is to say, religious belief seems to pose an obstacle to the inexorable process of the global domination of Western modernity.

I would argue, however, that ultimately belief and culture occupy strikingly similar positions in relationship to modernity. Indeed, where culture and belief diverge is largely in the imagination of Western liberalism, where the loss of some putative realm of unalienated culture is a source of sadness, while the idea of an unalienated belief system causes consternation and worry. The West deals with the critique suggested by both culture and belief by wishing for the existence of two self-canceling and impossible ideas: authentic culture and reified belief.

The idea of "real" belief as an other to modernity is encapsulated in the Weberian idea of modernity as a process of disenchantment. But Weber also conceptualized Protestantism as functioning at the very center of the transition to capitalist modernity. In other words, it is absurd to claim, as Dawkins does, that religion is in some way *exterior to* Western modernity.[36] Indeed, it seems possible to see it as functioning both as its occasional buttress and as a significant element of its loyal opposition: as part of a strain of heterogeneous critique of the reifications and rationalizations of modernity—in the name of human emancipation—that might well exist under the generalized name "romanticism."[37] Even modern fundamentalisms and neo-orthodox religious movements bear out this general point in the very complexity of their relationship to modernity. While many such movements base their appeal in a recoil from the perceived corruptions and degradations of modern life, many—for example, Reverend Moon's Unification Church, televangelists like Pat Robertson, the suburban U.S. superchurches, or the Orthodox Jewish Lubavitchers—also employ cutting-edge technologies and sophisticated techniques of the mainstream mass media in their worship and proselytizing activities. They are not, in other words, antimodernists (like, say, the Amish) so much as "reactionary modernists," fully imbricated with the sociopolitical systems, technologies, and ideologies of Western modernity.[38] Indeed, like cultures, belief systems today are creatures of the new modes of communication, commerce, and travel attendant upon the accelerated modernity we call globalization.

It is perhaps this sense of religion's complexly oppositional position in relation to modernity that accounts for some of its current cachet. Indeed, in a moment of apparently seamless neoliberal expansion, religious belief's frequent association with a romantic resistance to modernity suddenly seems newly significant.[39] For Žižek, the modern condition entails a "formal freedom" to make an array of ultimately meaningless choices: between consumer goods, political parties, and even identities in the supposedly free play of cyberspace. Against this inconsequential freedom to choose more of the same is the assertion of "actual freedom": the freedom to evade the existing power structure, neoliberal hegemony itself.[40] Religion is thus interesting to Žižek insofar as he sees all experiences of the sacred as instances of "unplugging" from the quotidian: "Is this 'unplugging' not simply the name for the basic ECSTATIC experience of entering the domain in which everyday rules are suspended, the domain of the sacred TRANSGRESSION?"[41] With his characteristic inversions of common sense, Žižek then finds some surprising resources for the project of actual freedom in both Jewish and Christian doctrine. Judaism becomes the religion in which adherence to religious law "unplugs" the believer from the daily life of one's surrounding community—and thereby, from the surcharge of emotion (and "guilt") associated with, for example, ethnic nationalism.[42] Christianity, then, represents not only a further transcendence of the law, but an assertion of "love as *jouissance* outside the Law."[43] Love, in turn, in his usage is (as opposed to desire) the relationship to an imperfect object: the Jesus who dies on the cross, or indeed the God who kills his own son. Ultimately, what Žižek calls for is an "unconditional engagement" with these religious (as opposed to ethical) injunctions: a detachment from the law as superego, and a commitment to this love of imperfect humanity/divinity.[44] Which is to say, we must accept the miraculous possibility that we can reinvent ourselves and the world.[45]

In this way, belief becomes for Žižek a way around (or better, through) the problem of difference, for the commitment to this version of faith entails universalism on several levels: that one's beliefs and actions are universally true and that everyone is a potential object of love. Indeed, one of Žižek's central theoretical goals is to demystify the other as the possessor of some secret Thing that makes him or her the obsessive object of desire/detestation: in his conception, we all bear the same Lacanian lack.[46] But Žižek's is also a very specific intervention into the idea of modernity. For Žižek, Christianity is the modern religion par excellence because it instantiates a break between ethics (moral norms) and religion, which entails both unconditional commitment and faith in the possibility of change. Christianity represents not only the historicity of breaks with the past but the promise of futurity. In other words, it is the religion of an emancipatory project that has yet to be completed: the universal project of modernity. To Dawkins and company, as well as to all those who go in for "decaffeinated" versions of belief, Žižek might reply that what's really needed is not less religious belief but more belief in modernity.[47]

CULTURE IN MODERNITY

Two problems present themselves at this point. First, what are the implications of endorsing a thoroughgoing modernity of the kind Žižek envisions, and second, where would such a project leave "culture"? Regarding the first question, we have to acknowledge its slightly heterodox quality, for certainly the idea of modernity has been charged with complicity in many of the worst features of the West's history of relationships with its others—indeed, of underwriting that very relationship of self and other. And yet, especially in light of Fish's observations about the ideology of the West as essentially being freedom from belief, one of the attractions of a wholesale commitment to modernity would precisely be the reinhabitation of that empty site at the heart of "our" belief system. Modernity is, as Gandhi famously said of Western civilization, "a very good idea": as good as any principle to commit to, good enough to wish for its actual existence.

Such belief in modernity resolves several problems for us. First, it allows us to break down the asymmetry between the West and the rest, by which the West exists in the universal truth of modernity, while the rest have their exotic beliefs. We may now say that the West has beliefs too, and precisely in the sense that we ascribe beliefs to others. These beliefs are *only* local and are situated in history and custom. Sometimes they comport with our various (and local) conceptions of rationality, and sometimes they don't: many of us still tell our kids about Santa Claus. Sometimes, as in the case of theologies or epistemologies, they bring with them their own complexly elaborated and internally consistent (that is, rational) systems. Our beliefs are tested by experience—sometimes rigorously and systematically, as in the case of scientific epistemology, but often far more haphazardly. Indeed, one such tested belief may well be our sense of the universality of Western civilization itself. In the crucible of imperialism and the global spread of capitalism, the West has been nothing if not successful in spreading elements of its social, economic, and religious systems, so the idea of a universal fit between humanity and the West has seemed like a reasonable hypothesis, internal contradictions aside. Only now, like the nineteenth-century American Millerites, who prophesied imminent Armageddon for year upon disappointed year, some simply continue to hold onto our belief in the exceptionality of Western modernity, against the mounting evidence. This kind of intellectual conservatism is probably part of the human repertoire as well. So is the expectation that if our beliefs are good for us then they must logically be good for others. Modernity, in other words, *is* cultural.

What, then, do we say to those who would wish to oppose Western modernity, or at least challenge its universal applicability? One response to this would be the Rortian point that, perhaps unfortunately, it doesn't matter what other people think about modernity: it is the belief system through and within which we coherently act.[48] If others organize their conceptual world via magic or a holy text, then they must do what they must as well. But this is an unsatisfying position in a number of respects. First, it returns us to a Huntingtonian vision of intractable antagonism between, say, Western civilization and whatever antimodern enemy it has lately conjured up—only now, ethnocentric arrogance is stiffened with a touch of fatalism. Or perhaps more precisely, it returns us to Fukuyama, who simply waved away "every crackpot messiah" who dared to object to the history-ending forces of liberalism, since ultimately "it matters very little what strange thoughts occur to people in Albania or Burkina Faso."[49] But more subtly, such a position also fails to address the fact that the idea of a thoroughgoing rejection of modernity is both terrifying and strangely exhilarating: terrifying in its sheer promise of conflictual alterity, yet wondrous in the way it promises to open up new, undreamed-of vistas of time, space, gods, and monsters.[50] We are returned to the issue of *desire* for such a position.

There are actually two desires here that are deeply intertwined. On the one hand, there is the desire for an outside to modern life that is as old and deep as modernity itself. This is the Romantic impulse that gave birth to anthropology and that now revolts at the idea that all are now incorporated into capitalist modernity, that all culture is reified. The other is a desire for a modernity that is yet to be: one that actually lives up to the promise of the freedom from traditional constraint implicit in the idea of Enlightenment, the "actual freedom" to which Žižek refers. And of course, these two desires are intertwined in that the desire to find modernity's outside is part of the revolt against the lived experience of modernity as an incomplete project. While we must now concede that modernity is cultural (that is, located within a specific social and historical context), culture is also the space where the gap between the formal freedom of neoliberal modernity and the actual freedom of Enlightenment is conceptualized. This is the precise reason why the idea of culture's reification by the forces of the modern market is so disturbing to some: it suggests the closure of that critical possibility.

CULTURE AND FUTURITY

In the face of the ubiquitous trivialization of culture—of difference—I acknowledge that it is often extremely hard any more to take the double perspective I have argued for here, considering the essentially *cultural* nature of modernity and the critical implications of culture in general. I will offer one final example of these ideas that will also lead seamlessly into the next chapter, on cultural rights.

Recent decades have seen a number of relatively high-budget fictional films set in the context of tribal societies. These include the Sami film *Ofelas* (*Pathfinder*, 1987); *Himalaya* (1999), which won a Best Foreign Film Oscar; the Inuit film *Atanarjuat* (*The Fast Runner*, 2001); and *Ten Canoes* (2006), set in Australia's Arnhem Land.[51] These films share enough features to almost be considered a genre. They all tell violent stories about conflicts among tribal members and thus both reference popular fiction film genres like the western and reply to the nonfiction ethnographic film tradition that tended to represent tribal societies' functionality.[52] But it is hard not to notice the way their mise-en-scène is also carefully arranged to emphasize their separateness from modernity. They are all set in remote and forbidding parts of the earth during a precontact ethnographic present.[53] The films are rendered in obscure languages, and they present elaborate customs and tales of relatively unfamiliar cultures. They speak to a desire to know and understand what it might have felt like to live outside modernity.

Yet to watch any of these films is also to witness a very modern act of cultural and linguistic survival; their very position outside modernity is, of course, also a separation from the scene of contact and colonialism. It is partly for this reason that Michelle Raheja has described *Atanarjuat,* with its self-consciously Inuit narrative, setting, cast, crew, and even production methods, as participating in an act of "visual sovereignty."[54] Though this can't plausibly be said of all of these films, it is nevertheless true that all do share significant participation from native writers, performers, translators, crew, and cultural consultants. Additionally, all the films are presented as ways of communicating important histories, values, and languages to future generations through the artifice of film. This is very clearly native culture reified, and indeed commodified, with the willing participation of those who wish it to be preserved. Nor is there anything mysterious about this process. Accompanying the DVD of *Ten Canoes* is a fascinating "Making of" documentary, which details Dutch-Australian director Rolf de Heer's original inspiration for the fictional film: the exhortations of his friend the Aboriginal actor David Gulpilil to make a film in Arnhem Land, and an encounter with a series of photographs taken in the 1930s of the Yolngu people by ethnographer Donald Thomson. These photographs became integral to the film in several ways. De Heer posed his actors to reproduce the historic photos; even the title image of the ten canoes came from a famous Thomson photo of ten Yolngu men crossing the Arafura Swamp. As the documentary reveals, Thomson's photos are also central in another way: they provided an important reference for the Yolngu crew and cast as they attempted to recreate the bark canoes central to both the film and the historical photo but no longer in much use in their community. According to the film's promotional materials, the ethnographer Thomson is a revered figure among the Yolngu, and "Thomson Time" is understood as a moment when the Yolngu people adhered to what they consider the traditional ways of life.[55]

This story should hold few surprises for us. The twists and turns of cultural use, borrowing, representation, intervention, invention, and collaboration have been a staple of ethnography for decades now. But why is the moral of this story so often about the inauthenticity and instability of culture as a category? For Peter Djigirr, the Yolngu co-director of the film *Ten Canoes*, the film's representation of traditional Yolngu culture had a different meaning:

> People, they always come, all those miners, and they ask us for mining and all that. But we come from this land. And we always tell them "No." But if we're going to do this film, and then they can recognize, all them white men. Recognize us. If we can't do this movie or this, all them Balanda (White) people, they can just come and come, they're putting us down now, because we'll be in bottom and at the top will be white man. But you people came here to lift up our futures. So after we die, maybe the new generation will grow up so they can see that picture where we're going and where they started from. That's what I want to see. To teach them. Because we don't want to lose our culture. Otherwise, if we go further, maybe white man can tell us, "Where's your culture? Nothing. You're lost. All bad luck for you."[56]

Djigirr's role in this film as co-director was to serve as a translator and cultural mediator between the Yolngu and the non-Aboriginal director and crew. If anyone, he would have had a complex understanding of the ways in which the film distilled the intercultural messiness of the production and interpretation process into a streamlined and simplified story—one that, like Thomson's famous photos before it, reifies Yolngu culture in a mythical prelapsarian moment. But rather than addressing this simplification, Djigirr is instead far more concerned to see the film as a reasonable response to his people's sense of impending obliteration in the face of the social and economic pressures of modernity: a way to fight back against both the miners and a white order that puts Aboriginal people at the bottom. In this sense, the film is for Djigirr an example of a process of externalization that allows Yolngu people not only to escape entering a cultureless "nothing" but to challenge and even change modernity as well. In the simplest sense, modernity must now "recognize": acknowledge the Yolngu not only as human beings but as humans who exist in the world in a certain way. This does not entail embracing or accepting all of their views. Rather, it requires an openness to the challenge that their (fully modern) cultural difference might present to the otherwise seeming sameness of neoliberal modernity.

CHAPTER 6

The Cultural Return

Having, in previous chapters, addressed some of the problems with the "against culture" position, we now turn to a more positive account of culture's continuing significance as a concept and category of analysis. To begin, I'll bring together the pieces of a definition of culture that I have been building in the preceding chapters, a culture that is at base dialectical and related to the larger problem of conceptualizing our current moment of neoliberal modernity. From there it should be clear how and why culture remains a central—that is, meaningful and non-trivial—analytical category for the coming years. But I also want to yoke this theoretical argument to what is to me one of the more compelling of the basic arguments for the centrality of cultural analysis: that this is a moment when various groups, globally, are clamoring for political and legal recognition and are invoking ideas of culture to do it. Given this fact, it is no surprise that, among academics, it is political scientists and philosophers who seem to be most likely these days to develop positive accounts of culture, in the terms of, say, liberal multicultural-ism and the idea of cultural rights. They are, in fact, directly engaged with culture as a problem, whether out of concern over the status of the neoliberal nation-state or the moral and political imperatives of the political recognition of minorities. For some time now liberal political philosophers have argued for the centrality of cultural belonging to accounts of justice in a liberal democracy.[1] I would like to examine this discussion but ultimately to argue for a more radical understanding of culture: one that shows its potentially corrosive power to challenge central tenets of neoliberal modernity.

THE CULTURAL DIALECTIC

To sum up, then. Culture as a concept has historically functioned in a number of registers. At its most abstract, culture is what mediates on a theoretical level between the universal and the particular, the real and the ideal. On the social level, it is what explains the connection between individuals and the groups to which they belong: families, communities, classes and castes, interest groups, national and transnational groups. It also explains the nature of the relationships between smaller and larger parts of a given social context: the relationship of families to villages; villages to regional, linguistic, or economic groupings; groups to more abstract alliances, such as those constituting national citizenship, political and class solidarities, religious affiliations, recreational clubs, and affinity groups. As such, it also denotes differences—between individuals and the various groups that compose social life as a whole. This is the first element of the dialectical nature of cultural discourse: that which accounts for the relationship of part to whole is also a term of differentiation.

On its largest scale, "culture" has come to be a central term in conceptualizations of modernity. Indeed, it is commonly said that culture emerged with the onset of modernity in the context of contact. In this moment, as in every instance of contact that has followed it, cultural difference was simultaneously invented and obliterated. In other words, particular cultures came into being only when they were encountered from the outside. But this encounter—the moment when the incorporation of the world's peoples into the capitalist global system began—would lead to the end of the very differences that were being observed. Henceforth, culture has served as a highly ambiguous sign of difference from modernity. While thinkers since Columbus have seen cultural difference as a site of critique of modernity from a variety of perspectives (nostalgic or futuristic, radical or conservative), we may perhaps best see culture as modernity's loyal opposition: the Romantic repository of all the other possible ways of living or imagining social life outside the dominant trend of history.

The cultural turn of the 1980s and 1990s represented but one particular historical moment in this ongoing dialectic of culture and modernity. Its historical context was the process of decolonization and the emergence of postnationalist antisystemic movements that allowed for the flourishing of new conceptions of culture as arrayed against the forces of midcentury modernity. The cultural turn's critique, then, allowed for the proliferation of theories and politics of identities, but it also enabled a rigorous debunking of older conceptions of culture that were tied to an earlier, nationalist, moment in the history of modernity. It is therefore no surprise that many critics in the cultural turn took to task the older notion of culture as excessively bounded, stable, and functional. In doing so, they reanimated the dialectic of culture and modernity by portraying culture as far more mobile, creative, and hybrid than previously imagined. The question before us now, in the face of the various critiques of both the cultural turn and culture itself, is whether this dialectic still remains analytically powerful.

The answer depends in great part on our understanding of our current geopolitical situation. But before turning to this topic, I must address one element of the cultural turn's project that I feel has indeed stalled. Whereas once it was vitally necessary to challenge a conception of cultures as a set of fixed, bounded, functional entities akin to a federation of nation-states, now this critique has led to a kind of theoretical paralysis, where generalizations of any kind, along with the intellectual project of totalization, are portrayed as conceptual errors. For this reason I have suggested at various points that we need to rethink the ban on reification. There are a number of ways to do this. The first entails recognizing that reification is fully one half of a dialectical process: the half that requires naming, systematization, synthesis. While thought must not be allowed to stop here, it nevertheless seems important to acknowledge the provisional significance of this kind of activity.

It is sometimes suggested that the very act of cultural naming (even self-naming) represents a kind of fall, permanently setting into stone the particular form and nature of a culture. But I don't find this a satisfying or accurate account of the desire for recognition on several counts. First, as a commonsensical point, we can easily conjure up examples of groups who have held tenaciously to their cultural identities while the specific content of that identity, all the practices and beliefs that it once connoted, have shifted. The Yolngu still see themselves as Yolngu even though they have largely forgotten how to make bark canoes and have lately taken to filmmaking. It doesn't necessarily follow, in other words, that the act of self-identification entails any codification of practices or beliefs at all.

But this is not to say that culture is content-neutral, or that a cultural self-identification entails no specific practices or beliefs. Rather, cultural self-identification represents an instance of the act of naming some people or a territory, a language, or a set of cherished beliefs and practices in a particular place and time. Cultural self-naming is an act of abstraction, of providing a name for a complex set of ideas, histories, associations, and needs. But this codification is only provisional; though a shaper of reality, it is also altered by historical change.

Many legitimate concerns have arisen about the way that reified conceptions of culture have been mobilized to justify the oppression of individuals or to heighten conflicts between groups. But it does not necessarily follow from this that the discrete act of cultural self-naming is itself suspect. That is, we may object to the way a conceptualization of culture is manipulated, or to the way it is codified by certain special interests or appropriated unfairly. But these harms are not intrinsic to the desire to be recognized culturally. The apposite distinction here—already provisionally offered in the last chapter—is between externalization *(Entaüsserung)* and alienation *(Veraüsserung)*. Marx acknowledged that the political economy of his predecessors, starting with Adam Smith, correctly recognized the fundamental centrality of labor as the essence of property, but he faulted them for forgetting the human nature of that labor.[2] The naming of a culture represents a similar act of externalization; only when that named culture connotes something outside the lived and evolving experience of real human beings does it become alienated. This challenge to the ban on cultural reification, I would argue, is more than just a theoretical refinement, and more even than just an attempt to cut through the ban on graven images that seems to have gripped fields like cultural anthropology.[3] For without it we may fail to see some of the contours of our own geopolitical context—a context, indeed, where culture and culturalist thought may be more central than ever.

GLOBAL MULTICULTURALISM

In chapter 3, I offered a history of the cultural turn that showed how it emerged out of a very different kind of political mood in the immediate postwar period. Then, in the face of the defeat of fascism and the thoroughly discredited deployment of culture that helped form its self-justification, the universalist discourse of human rights understandably gained in political significance. And yet culture, in many respects a product of American social science, emerged somewhat uncomfortably as a challenge to this universalism, only to develop its full power in the struggles of the 1960s. Indeed, we can take the civil rights movement as the premier example of this shift. While the idea of civil rights was initially a clear extension of the universalist conception of human rights (rights that had been unfairly denied to one group of humans on the basis of race), as the movement evolved it took on familiar lineaments of cultural particularism, especially when its adherents began questioning the extent to which working for a color-blind justice would achieve their larger goals of combating racism in all corners of society. Thus the universalist aspirations of the civil rights movement were answered with the culturalist orientation of, for example, Black Power and the Black Arts movement. This view that the achievement of human equality and justice was not just a juridical problem to be solved through a fairer application of universal standards but a *cultural* one, to be addressed at the level of the individual and the group through consciousness raising, political art and theater, education, historical recovery projects, and so forth, spread throughout the antisystemic movements of the 1960s and 1970s.

Of course, this division between universalist and culturalist perspectives and approaches within antisystemic movements can be blamed for some of the more notorious internal splits in various movements as well: the rancorous divisions, for example, between liberal, radical, and cultural feminists.[4] But to focus on this is also to miss the extent to which *both* universalism and culturalism have permeated and changed official social structures and institutions in profound ways. On the universalist side, we can point to the emergence of the international human rights regime and, more abstractly, to the political power of concepts like human rights and equal citizenship.[5] On the particularist side of things, we have seen how acceding to these universalist ideas often requires acknowledgment of the specific histories and situations of minorities. Thus both universalism and particularism are reflected in such events as Australia's official apology for the nation's treatment of Aboriginal peoples, or in the fact that the European Union monitors a nation's treatment of its internal minorities before admitting that nation to membership status. According to Will Kymlicka, in various international political bodies, "ideas of multiculturalism and minority rights, which one might have expected to be relegated to the peripheral institutions of the international community dealing with 'culture' and 'heritage,' have permeated the core institutions relating to security, development, and human rights."[6]

An interesting, if fraught, example of the extent to which minority and indigenous rights have permeated the concept of human rights internationally was in the opening ceremonies of the 2008 Beijing Olympics, which included a parade of children dressed in regional Chinese minority costumes and holding an enormous Chinese flag. A minor scandal ensued when it was subsequently revealed in the foreign press that the costumed children were misrepresented as members of minority groups; they all belonged to the Han ethnic majority.[7] But the fact that the Chinese, long averse to the very idea of the presence of internal minorities, included such a display in this, their international "coming-out party," and the fact that they were perceived as having been deceptive, speaks volumes about the state of international norms regarding minority recognition.[8] Chinese authorities clearly understood that a display of minority recognition was a sign of the nation's acquiescence to international standards of human rights. Similarly, observers' outrage over this minor deception seemingly served to confirm China's history of human rights failures.

Of course, much attention (in this book and elsewhere) has been given to the idea that we are in the midst of a backlash against such ideas as multiculturalism, and insofar as the term refers internationally to an extremely diverse set of issues—from curricular reform in the United States to questions regarding immigration in Australia, to religious accommodation in parts of Europe—it is clear that "multiculturalism" has taken on a pejorative edge.[9] But I am tempted to take this backlash as a sign not of the failure of the cultural turn but of its very institutionalization. A salient example here is the British New Right's direct reliance on the formulations of cultural studies to produce a new nationalist, anti-immigrant rhetoric.[10] Similarly, the American resistance to a multiculturalism strongly associated with the education establishment cannot be entirely separated from a long political history of populist anti-intellectualism.

Just as it is important to distinguish between older forms of racism and contemporary manifestations of prejudice, it is also important to contextualize the apparent current backlash against cultural recognition. Kymlicka, a central theorist of liberal multiculturalism, has observed that in many cases backlash against cultural recognition falls disproportionately against new minorities (namely immigrants), and has thus been particularly virulent lately in western Europe, which has a shorter history of mass immigration than the settler colonies of Canada, the United States, Australia, and New Zealand, and where (as in the case of France) ideologies of national-cultural uniformity are strongly held. But even in the face of this backlash, and the various concomitant calls for a return to universalism, there has been a significant shift in international politics toward recognizing indigenous peoples and historic minorities (those, such as the Basques or the Québécois, who have long held minority status in their respective nation-states).[11] We see this bifurcation in the politics of recognition in, for example, the United Kingdom, where rancorous debates over immigrants' desires for separate accommodations for culture and religion can be juxtaposed to the activity and relative legitimacy of the Scots, Welsh, and Cornish separatist movements. A petition was recently put before the UN to have the Crofters of the Scottish Highlands and islands officially designated an indigenous people.[12] In other words, if we bracket the contentious issue of immigrants' cultural rights and focus on those of indigenous peoples and historical minorities, we see the dramatic extent to which culturalist ideas have permeated both the international political and legal frameworks and people's day-to-day sense of their social worlds.

In sum, it may be possible to account for the cultural turn of the 1980s and 1990s as precisely that moment in which the culturalist perspectives of the antisystemic movements of the postwar period became formalized. That is, they found their way into established institutional structures of all kinds, including education, national and international legal systems, and political systems. But in the face of this development, the distinctive challenges and features of the 1980s and 1990s also reinforced the centrality of the idea of culture. A period often identified with the end of the cold war and the beginning of neoliberal globalization, it was defined by dramatic shifts in the geopolitical order: on the one hand by the rise of such supranational entities as the European Union, the World Bank, and the International Monetary Fund and on the other by the emergence of ethnic conflict and the devolution of former nation-states including Yugoslavia, Czechoslovakia, and the USSR. In other words, the stereotypically homogenizing, universalizing tendencies of globalization were accompanied by the breakdown of older political entities into smaller units. Cultural particularism was, from the beginning, a central feature of neoliberal globalization.

It is in part for this reason that Saskia Sassen prefers to regard globalization as a process of "denationalization." Rather than being a matter of the emergence of vast new global powers and entities destined to sweep away the nation-state, or even a renegotiation of relations between nations, globalization is for Sassen something that was set in place *within* the older global order of strong nation-states. In particular, she argues, neoliberal globalization has entailed dramatic internal transformations within nations regarding conceptions of territory, political authority, and the rights of citizens.[13] From a perspective such as this we may fully see not only the extent to which "culture" persists as a fundamental term in this process but the extent to which culturalist thought remains a central analytic for understanding our present. For in fact, in a number of ways we may see the cultural turn as a feature of denationalization. The cultural turn's postnational revision of the culture concept became a key analytic precisely because it offered a way to understand some of the processes of denationalization under way in global neoliberalism. Correspondingly, the institutionalization of culture was itself a symptom of denationalization; "culture" became— and continues to be—a key term for thinking about the transformations within nations regarding territory, authority, and rights. But we may also understand the backlash against culture within this frame. Certainly, agendas resisting culture and culturalism in order to return to the verities of older forms of modernity reflect a general discomfort with the current denationalized state of modernity. Meanwhile, those who fret over "culture's" misuses and reifications are centrally reacting to the term's institutionalization and hence, implicitly, to its loss of critical power in the dialectic of culture and modernity. Because I consider this latter concern in some ways the most compelling, I would like to offer, in the remaining pages, a description of the way that culture may yet operate in critical and even transformative ways in our denationalizing present.

CULTURE AND DENATIONALIZATION

"Denationalization" refers to a number of processes that have generally been identified with globalization, including the privatization of various formerly state functions such as the maintenance of prisons, roads, and the military; financial deregulation; the establishment of international organizations that take over former state functions, such as the International Criminal Court and the World Bank; the emergence of new classes of mobile cosmopolitan subjects; and the development of apparently extraterritorial spaces like the Internet and global finance. But unlike the idea of globalization, which has tended to emphasize a transcendence of the particularities of nation-states in a global homogeneity, denationalization focuses on the ways in which national structures are integral to globalization: that is, nations both facilitate these processes of globalization and are changed by it. Thus denationalization is also characterized by a dramatically changed organization of governance: in the United States in the Bush-Cheney regime, for example, political power was in effect "privatized" by being increasingly arrogated to a secretive executive branch.[14]

Importantly for our interests, the state's relationship to citizens is also dramatically transformed. Some of this has to do with the privatization of political power and the withdrawal of the welfare state, so that nations have less direct involvement with their citizens' lives, and citizens, in turn, feel less beholden to the state. But it also pertains to complex changes in legal citizenship and rights brought about by global migrations. For the privileged, these changes amount to a "flexible citizenship," in which individuals finesse the constraints of state sovereignty and national and ethnic identity to optimize their ability to work in the international spaces of commerce.[15] But for the vast numbers of less privileged migrant workers, citizenship rights are also being significantly transformed. While their mobility often comes with the price of a curtailment of citizens' rights, there are also interesting examples of new arrangements of rights emerging in their place. Some countries of origin are allowing emigrant citizens to vote, while in some host countries migrants are acquiring more localized rights—say, property rights, rights to national identity cards, or, as in amnesty agreements, opportunities to accede to full citizenship.[16] On a more conceptual level, one also sees the loosening relationship between sovereign nations and the idea of citizenship in recent coinages like "environmental citizenship," which directly refer to an inter-nesting set of allegiances and obligations that scale from local practices to the entire planet.[17]

We may see that, in a general sense, culture becomes a useful optic for understanding these new arrangements of citizenship, at least insofar as it capaciously describes the border-defining practices of identity and recognition that are made so visible in our current political moment. But perhaps a more direct example of the way culture is in play in denationalization occurs in the context of the international human rights regime. Within its universalizing discourse, a particularist countercurrent of "cultural rights" has emerged, as a kind of right that significantly transforms our ways of understanding state sovereignty, its territorial authority, and its relationship to its citizens.

The Obama administration has provided some historic political theater that dramatically represents elements of this change in the relationship between states, territories, and citizens. In 2009, the first annual White House Tribal Nations Conference, billed as the largest gathering of tribal leaders in U.S. history, promised leaders of recognized tribes an opportunity to address the entrenched problems facing Indian Country directly with leaders and administrators in the federal government. Whatever its ultimate efficacy in creating significant change in some of the most impoverished communities in the United States, the conference at the very least offered an interesting restaging of the traditional motif of Indian leaders traveling to Washington to sign over rights in the form of deceptive treaties and to pay obeisance to the sovereign power. The president himself (recently adopted into the Crow Nation) offered himself up in the service to native peoples—indeed, as one of them: to significant applause, Obama joked, "Only in America could the adoptive son of Crow Indians grow up to become President of the United States."[18]

This theater of tribal sovereignty and power would only continue in the second such conference in 2010, when Obama used the occasion to announce the United States' support of the 2007 UN Declaration on the Rights of Indigenous Peoples. Like New Zealand and Canada, the United States had been a holdout against this declaration, ostensibly because of language that strongly asserted indigenous rights to traditional lands and resources. But the declaration's attack on national sovereignty goes far beyond asserting indigenous rights to property. Indeed, it fully conforms to the logic of denationalization, asserting, for example, "the inherent rights of indigenous peoples which derive from their political, economic and social structures and from their cultures, spiritual traditions, histories and philosophies, especially their rights to their lands, territories and resources," and declaring that "the rights affirmed in treaties, agreements and other constructive arrangements between States and indigenous peoples are, in some situations, matters of international concern, interest, responsibility and character."[19] As holders of rights autonomously derived from "their cultures," and as persons whose conditions are "matters of international concern," indigenous peoples are thus doubly removed from the power of the traditional nation-state.

The 2007 UN Declaration is nonbinding: that is, it will not supersede national laws, and this is probably why the United States will finally become a party to it. Nevertheless, this announcement has provoked a new right-wing conspiracy theory that Obama plans to sell Manhattan back to the Indians.[20] And, as is the case with most conspiracy theories, there is a distorted kernel of truth buried here: that, though the language of this declaration is far more specific in its support of the rights of indigenous peoples than ever before, it is entirely in keeping with the trend of the international law of human rights that has enabled some impressive victories for indigenous peoples over both state and corporate power.

The ideas in this document are in many ways only amplifications of concepts that have been embryonically part of the international law of human rights since the 1948 UN Universal Declaration of Human Rights. Perhaps most importantly, these concepts were codified in the 1966 International Covenant on Economic, Social, and Cultural Rights, which, as of the beginning of 2011, has been ratified by 160 countries. The 1966 Covenant asserts that "all peoples have the right of self-determination. By virtue of that right they freely determine their political status and freely pursue their economic, social and cultural development" and that "the States Parties to the present Covenant recognize the right of everyone . . . to take part in cultural life."[21] Because this Covenant has the status of a treaty, it is cited in national case law and has been used, for example, to support efforts to protect Canadian First Nations' land use claims, Maori fishing rights in New Zealand, and Sami reindeer husbandry in Finland—often against large corporate mining and timber interests.[22] This kind of case law, in turn, has contributed to the acceptance of the idea that cultural resources, like environmental resources, are deserving of protection. Native Hawaiians, for example, have been partially successful in challenging the U.S. military's use of an area in Oahu on the grounds that it is both environmentally and culturally sensitive—which in the latter case means not only that the region has archaeological significance but that access to it and its resources is vital to the perpetuation of native Hawaiian culture.[23]

The concept of cultural rights has come up for criticism in what should be to attentive readers some predictable ways. For starters, it runs against the grain of orthodox liberal political theory, which emphasizes juridical egalitarianism and especially individualism.[24] In a related vein, some object to the concept's potentially corrosive effect on universalist notions of human rights and on the rights of individuals upon whom a cultural designation is imposed.[25] For these critics, the specter of collective rights of any kind brings up a predictable set of horror scenarios: the establishment of hierarchies of groups, as in apartheid; or transgressions of individual (especially women's) rights, as exemplified by such practices as female genital mutilation, forced marriage, domestic violence, and the veil.[26] For some of these critics, and many others, cultural rights as an idea is insufficiently nuanced regarding the way in which groups, and relations among groups, are conceptualized. Some will argue that the idea of cultural rights represents yet another reification of cultural complexity, enshrining a stable and static idea of cultures within the law. Those who concern themselves over this problem will often address the ethnographic complexity of both indigenous conceptions of group formation and the partial or unstable way in which these mesh with the kind of cultural rights recognition envisioned by the international human rights regime.[27]

The concern about cultural rights as a substantial challenge to a universalist conception of human rights is a complex point to which a great deal of critical attention has been given.[28] But here I would proceed by suggesting that this problem is in fact a variant of the issue addressed in the last chapter, whereby culture is too often understood as alien to and outside modernity—a modernity, in turn, that presents itself as universal. So as before, I would argue instead for understanding group rights and universal human rights as dialectically and historically interrelated. For an example of this point, one need only consider Kymlicka's important observation that several of the most important classic liberal accounts of human rights tacitly acknowledge collective identity and "cultural membership" as central to liberals' conception of human agency. But this collective formation, which Kymlicka identifies as nothing less than the nation-state, goes largely unspecified for the precise and deeply historical reason that its centrality has been so thoroughly taken for granted.[29]

This, in turn, should point us to the historicity of the idea of cultural rights and to its possibilities. While cultural rights are clearly a product of the specific context of denationalization, the concept of cultural rights has the potential to expand our understanding of human rights, much the way that cultural thought once expanded the idea of the human. But I also want to argue, perhaps perversely, that in this context there is a specific advantage in a discourse of culture, which is precisely derived from the historical slipperiness and complexity of the term.

THE CASE FOR SLIPPERINESS

I should be clear. By celebrating slipperiness and complexity, I am not endorsing a version of culture as an endless play of contested, hybrid, and mobile spaces. Descriptively, it may be all that. But I also want to hold open the idea that for many people the experience of having a culture is a powerfully felt affirmation of self and community. It is because of the widely recognized resonance with this emotion that the idea of culture as itself a good to be protected and promoted has gained such traction in many political arenas. And because of this, it is also now a tool that is being very deliberately—sometimes cannily, sometimes disastrously—wielded in the contestations of power that constitute our current political moment. Obviously, neither getting rid of the idea of culture nor refining it into a theoretically tolerable abstraction will resolve the conflicts that emerge from its deployment. The slipperiness and complexity, then, are nothing less than those of the political realm itself, whereby—and especially in a moment of denationalization—competing definitions of culture have increasingly come to join competing definitions of rights, virtues, and obligations. To put this in more concrete terms, I would urge those who might even be tempted to entertain such a question as "Is Multiculturalism Bad for Women?" to instead rethink the question dramatically: How do women, collectively and as individuals, become formed by, exist within, embrace, deploy, engage with, resist, and change their cultural contexts?[30]

But let me give an even more concrete example that explicitly returns culture to the public sphere of law. NAGPRA, the Native American Grave Protection and Repatriation Act, stipulates that both human remains and "cultural patrimony," as it is called, be returned from museums and other collections to U.S. native peoples. To be designated part of a people's cultural patrimony and therefore considered for repatriation, some of the following criteria have to apply: the object is understood to be collectively owned; it is seen to have a clear relationship with the religious practices of the group; it is authentic (meaning, apparently, both that it is not a replica and that it is in some ways typical of and specific to the group); and (and this obviously follows from some of the rest of these ideas) it has a certain value that isn't simply reducible to monetary worth.[31]

These criteria are interesting on a number of grounds. On the one hand, in their emphasis on collective ownership and unquantifiable value, they fly in the face of the individualism and reification at the core of modern capitalism. On the other hand, they can readily be seen as enshrining a bounded and static conception of culture, as well as age-old stereotypes of indigenous peoples as inherently religious, group-thinking, traditional, outside history, and so forth. But it turns out that in its actual deployment in the decisions of cases, the stereotypical assumptions the law seems to enshrine are often surprisingly upended. Not only have the Kwakiutl gotten back potlatch items that have a clear and intensely individual ownership history, but the Zuñi have had repatriated a collection of Christian missionary art, and the Minnesota Chippewa have gotten back some British flags and peace medals. In other words, on a case-by-case basis, neither issues of personal ownership, nor those of history, nor questions of religious or cultural authenticity have impeded the repatriation process. Indeed, in the Zuñi case, it seems that the central deciding issue was the fact that the objects had clearly been stolen.[32] So there is a larger observation to make here about the way the legal system, at least, addresses the idea of culture. Not only does it not *necessarily* engage in reifications and stereotyping, especially when a body of cases are considered in aggregate, but, since it operates on a case-by-case basis, within specific circumstances and with different people making the decisions, there is a great deal of play in how things get defined, the relative weight given to specific questions, and so forth. Given this flexibility, the fact that we are so often undecided about the exact meaning of a key concept like culture—or indeed, a concept like cultural property—might in fact be not so much the kind of conceptual mess we sometimes think it to be but rather a site of possibility, and a site that is responsive to an evolving body of law and changing public opinion. This point is, by the way, not original to me; it has also been made with regard to the international context of cultural rights.[33] Put more abstractly, the emergence of these kinds of figures into political and legal thought has allowed not only for individual examples of justice but for subtle—and perhaps not-so-subtle—challenges to long-held conventional beliefs.

Though first codified in international law in 1966, it is only in the context of the end of the cold war that considerations of cultural rights have emerged with significant force. Obviously, nation-states continue to be the central grantors and guarantors of rights, including cultural rights, but the issues presented by migration and globalization and the emergence of extranational legal and political entities have mightily challenged older accepted notions of internal homogeneity and international obligation. The desire for a concept like cultural rights speaks not only to the positive sense of group membership to which many people respond but also to the desire for a new way to consider questions of belonging and obligation without necessarily conceding the centrality of the homogeneous nation-state. The situation of so-called fourth-world peoples is thus particularly salient for thinking through some of these issues related to denationalization. In some cases, this is because of their already peculiar legal statuses in relation to nations, as internally colonized semisovereign populations or as traversers of national borders. Then too, as I mentioned in the previous chapter, indigenous groups have entered the world stage, forming international alliances with other such groups and developing ways to leverage their relationships with national authorities by appealing to extranational entities and interests. Thus, for example, Amazonian Indians have continued to appeal successfully to international environmentalists and others to demand social services and fight logging, mining, and hydropower in the rainforest.[34] Additionally, indigenous people have emerged as stakeholders in the face of an unprecedented trend in intellectual property law to vastly extend patent, copyright, and trademark protections to such things as symbols, folklore, traditional knowledge, and even forms of life.[35]

It would be tempting to celebrate the small victories of indigenous groups to take and retain control of various tangible and intangible resources—especially when they are going up against powerful multinational corporations. But that would likely both overstate the efficacy of these kinds of struggles and the purity of the motives of the parties involved. For every Amazonian Indian whose claim to land rights is linked to preserving the Amazonian canopy, there are plenty of examples in which indigenous assertions of hunting and fishing rights have run afoul of environmentalists' goals. Rather, what I am interested in here is the emergent and unsettled nature of this situation, in which the consequences of various ideas have yet to emerge. What is the future of an idea like cultural property, with its emphasis on ownership (what is ownership?) by a collective, whose very composition and definition are inherently in flux? What is the future of an idea like *intangible* cultural property, and how does it potentially complicate the very notion of intellectual property as currently understood? And what, finally, about cultural rights, with its implications about the meaning of personhood itself, as not only a rights-bearing being but an entity defined through a multiplicity of possible collective identifications and associations? Returning to culture with these kinds of questions in mind, we will be fully in dialogue with the future.

Notes

INTRODUCTION

1. Jonathan Franzen, *The Corrections* (New York: Picador, 2001), 44.
2. Ibid., 45.
3. Ibid., 92.
4. Ibid., 115.
5. Christian Joppke, "The Retreat of Multiculturalism in the Liberal State: Theory and Policy," *British Journal of Sociology* 55, no. 2 (2004): 237–57; Anne Phillips, *Multiculturalism without Culture* (Princeton: Princeton University Press, 2007); Susan Hegeman, "Shopping for Identities: 'A Nation of Nations' and the Weak Ethnicity of Objects," *Public Culture* 3, no. 2 (Spring 1991): 71–92.
6. Retort [collective consisting of Iain Boal, T. J. Clark, Joseph Matthews, and Michael Watts], *Afflicted Powers: Capital and Spectacle in a New Age of War*, new ed. (New York: Verso, 2006), 9.
7. But see David Harvey's powerful reconsideration of primitive accumulation as "accumulation by dispossession." For Harvey, the kind of accumulation of resources theorized by Marx as primitive accumulation is understood to be not just an initial criterion for the development of capitalism but an ongoing process and an engine of capitalist growth and development. David Harvey, *The New Imperialism* (New York: Oxford University Press, 2003) and *Spaces of Global Capitalism* (New York: Verso, 2006).
8. Uniting these trends is a return, more specifically, to Kant. See Alain Badiou, *Ethics: An Essay on the Understanding of Evil*, trans. Peter Hallward (New York: Verso, 2001), 1–3, 8. For key texts on the turn to aesthetics, see Elaine Scarry, *On Beauty and Being Just* (Princeton: Princeton University Press, 1999); George Levine, ed. *Aesthetics and Ideology* (New Brunswick: Rutgers University Press, 1994); Wendy Steiner, *Venus in Exile: The Rejection of Beauty*

in Twentieth-Century Art (New York: Free Press, 2001). For a brief overview of the return to "beauty" in art criticism, see Alexander Alberro, "Beauty Knows No Pain," *Art Journal* 63, no. 2 (Summer 2004): 36–43. The most influential figures in the return to ethics are Emmanuel Lévinas and Martha Nussbaum; on the return to theology, see Paul J. Griffiths, "The Very Idea of Religion," *First Things* 103 (May 2000): 30–35.

9. Marjorie Levinson's generous survey of the "new formalism" links its polemical energies to a repudiation of new historicism; Levinson, "What Is New Formalism?" *PMLA* 122, no. 2 (March 2007): 558–69. In an MLA presidential address, Marjorie Perloff approvingly quotes Terry Eagleton's view that formal literary analysis is being lost in the face of the preeminence of "content analysis"; Perloff, "Presidential Address 2006: It Must Change," *PMLA* 122, no. 3 (May 2007): 658. See also George Levine, "Introduction: Reclaiming the Aesthetic," in *Aesthetics and Ideology*, 1–30. On cinephilia, see Jonathan Rosenbaum and Adrian Martin, eds., *Movie Mutations: The Changing Face of World Cinephilia* (London: BFI, 2003); and Christian Keathley, *Cinephilia and History, or The Wind in the Trees* (Bloomington: Indiana University Press, 2005).

10. Jonathan Loesberg offers an especially subtle example of the disciplinary argument, calling for a turn toward formalism not simply for the sake of returning to some core disciplinary object or method but as a "voluntary askesis" of "disciplinary enclosure" for the purposes of opening up anew the question of the relationship of form to content and history; Loesberg, "Cultural Studies, Victorian Studies, and Formalism," *Victorian Literature and Culture* 27 (1999): 540. As Perloff also exemplifies, such calls for "new formalism" also have other agendas, including the reestablishment of canonical literature and especially lyric poetry (displaced since the moment of New Criticism) at the center of literary scholarship. Levinson connects new formalism with the "striking interest in metrical study observable over the past decade." Marjorie Levinson, "What Is New Formalism?," 568 n. 1; see also her "Appendix B (Metrical Study)," in "What Is New Formalism (Long Version)," http://sitemaker.umich.edu/pmla_article/home, August 21, 2007; and Charles Altieri, "Taking Lyrics Literally: Teaching Poetry in a Prose Culture," *New Literary History* 32, no. 2 (Spring 2001): 259–81.

11. See Levinson, "What Is New Formalism?"; and Perloff, "Presidential Address."

12. See Loesberg, "Cultural Studies."

13. For discussions (and demolitions) of these oppositions, see respectively Bruce Robbins, "Presentism, Pastism, Professionalism," *Victorian Literature and Culture* 27 (1999): 457–63; and Isobel Armstrong, "Victorian Studies and Cultural Studies: A False Dichotomy," *Victorian Literature and Culture* 27 (1999): 513–16.

14. John Guillory, for example, marks cultural studies' alleged disciplinary overreaching as ending with Alan Sokal's 1996 hoax against the editors of the cultural studies journal *Social Text*. Guillory portrays the journal's investment in science studies as a salvo in the ongoing conflict between the two competing academic fields of the sciences and humanities: "The stakes in this conflict were

not in any profound sense philosophical but rather disciplinary: the possibility of an alliance between cultural studies and science studies. If that alliance had been successful, criticism stood to advance its effort to recover the human world as its proper object even while undercutting the basis for the *scientific* study of that world. But the Sokal affair turned the tide of this battle in another direction." John Guillory, "The Sokal Affair and the History of Criticism," *Critical Inquiry* 28, no. 2 (2002): 483.

15. Alberro, "Beauty Knows No Pain," 43.

16. Badiou, *Ethics*, 5–6.

17. See Steiner, *Venus in Exile*.

18. Christopher Castiglia and Russ Castronovo, "A 'Hive of Subtlety': Aesthetics and the End(s) of Cultural Studies," *American Literature* 76, no. 3 (September 2004): 428; and see Alberro, "Beauty Knows No Pain," for a similar point about "humanist aesthetics": "It no longer sees art's pursuit of transcendence in dialectical tension with the quest for knowledge, understanding, and the improvement of our contemporary condition. Rather, it is now solely in the most personal, fleeting, and insubstantial facets of experience—namely, in the aesthetic and only in the aesthetic—that humans are seen to be able to come together in keeping with one another" (43).

19. See, for example, Jacques Rancière, *The Politics of Aesthetics* (New York: Continuum, 2004); and Marjorie Garber, Beatrice Hanssen, and Rebecca L. Walkowitz, eds., *The Turn to Ethics* (New York: Routledge, 2000).

20. Similarly, Levinson usefully distinguishes between two forms of new formalism: "activist formalism," which seeks "to restore to today's reductive reinscription of historical reading its original focus on form," and "normative formalism," which aims to "bring back a sharp demarcation between history and art, discourse and literature"; Levinson, "What Is New Formalism?," 559. On the pedagogical dimensions of this "normative" formalism, see Altieri, "Taking Lyrics Literally."

21. Fredric Jameson, *A Singular Modernity: Essay on the Ontology of the Present* (New York: Verso, 2002), 177.

22. Ibid., 178.

23. Ibid.

24. Ibid.

25. See, for example, Lila Abu-Lughod, "Writing against Culture," in *Recapturing Anthropology*, ed. Richard G. Fox (Santa Fe, NM: School of American Research Press, 1991), 137–62; Virginia Dominguez, "The Messy Side of 'Cultural Politics,'" *South Atlantic Quarterly* 91, no. 1 (Winter 1992): 19–42; Walter Benn Michaels, *Our America: Nativism, Modernism, and Pluralism* (Durham: Duke University Press, 1995); Joel S. Kahn, "Culture: Demise or Resurrection?," *Critique of Anthropology* 9, no. 2 (Autumn 1989): 33–51; Johannes Fabian, "Culture, Time, and the Object of Anthropology," in *Time and the Work of Anthropology: Critical Essays, 1971–91* (Philadelphia: Harwood Academic Publishers, 1991); Adam Kuper, *Culture: The Anthropologist's Account* (Cambridge, MA: Harvard University Press, 1999).

26. See James Clifford, *The Predicament of Culture: Twentieth-Century Ethnography, Literature, and Art* (Cambridge, MA: Harvard University Press,

1988), 235–36; Renato Rosaldo, *Culture and Truth: The Remaking of Social Analysis* (Boston: Beacon Press, 1989); Arjun Appadurai, *Modernity at Large: Cultural Dimensions of Globalization* (Minneapolis: University of Minnesota Press, 1996).

27. For example, David Scott objects that a poststructuralist culture concept "underwrites a liberal conception of how differences are to be viewed and regulated." Many Marxists have complained that "culture" has become too all-encompassing and that it obscures aspects of struggle or political engagement. David Scott, "Culture in Political Theory," *Political Theory* 31, no. 1 (February 2003): 92–115; Terry Eagleton, *The Idea of Culture* (Oxford: Blackwell, 2000).

28. For critical responses to calls to reject "culture," see Robert Brightman, "Forget Culture: Replacement, Transcendence, Relexification," *Cultural Anthropology* 10, no. 4 (November 1995): 509–46; and Christoph Brumann, "Writing for Culture: Why a Successful Concept Should Not Be Discarded," *Current Anthropology* 40, suppl. 1 (1999): S1–27.

29. Among the many interesting works that take the Boasian tradition to be instructive for the contemporary theory and practice of anthropology are Ira Bashkow et al., "A New Boasian Anthropology: Theory for the 21st Century," *American Anthropologist* 106, no. 3 (2004): 433–34; Ira Bashkow, "A Neo-Boasian Concept of Cutural Boundaries," *American Anthropologist* 106, no. 3 (2004): 443–58; Matti Bunzl, "Boas, Foucault, and The 'Native Anthropologist': Notes toward a Neo-Boasian Anthropology," *American Anthropologist* 106, no. 3 (2004): 435–68; Regna Darnell, *Invisible Genealogies: A History of Americanist Anthropology* (Lincoln: University of Nebraska Press, 2001); and Richard Handler, *Critics against Culture: Anthropological Observers of Mass Society* (Madison: University of Wisconsin Press, 2005). For interdisciplinary treatments of the Boasian tradition, see, for example, Brad Evans, *Before Cultures: The Ethnographic Imagination in American Literature, 1865–1920* (Chicago: University of Chicago Press, 2005); Susan Hegeman, *Patterns for America: Modernism and the Concept of Culture* (Princeton: Princeton University Press, 1999); and Marc Managanaro, *Culture, 1922: The Emergence of a Concept* (Princeton: Princeton University Press, 2002).

30. Michael F. Brown, *Who Owns Native Culture?* (Cambridge, MA: Harvard University Press, 2003), 218.

31. Richard G. Fox and Barbara J. King, "Introduction: Beyond Culture Worry," in *Anthropology beyond Culture*, ed. Richard G. Fox and Barbara J. King (New York: Berg, 2002), 1–19.

32. Victoria E. Bonnell and Lynn Hunt, eds., *Beyond the Cultural Turn: New Directions in the Study of Society and Culture* (Berkeley: University of California Press, 1999).

33. Michael Denning, *Culture in the Age of Three Worlds* (New York: Verso, 2004); see also Imre Szeman, "Culture and Globalization, or, the Humanities in Ruins," *CR: The New Centennial Review* 3, no. 2 (Summer 2003): 91–115.

34. See Sherry B. Ortner, introduction to *The Fate of "Culture": Geertz and Beyond*, ed. Sherry B. Ortner (Berkeley: University of California Press, 1999), 1–13.

35. See James Clifford and George E. Marcus, eds., *Writing Culture: The Poetics and Politics of Ethnography* (Berkeley: University of California Press, 1986); and, for an example of the literary scholar's interest in ethnography, Janice A. Radway, *A Feeling for Books: The Book-of-the Month Club, Literary Taste, and Middle-Class Desire* (Chapel Hill: University of North Carolina Press, 1997).

36. Nicholas B. Dirks, "In Near Ruins: Cultural Theory at the End of the Century," in *In Near Ruins: Cultural Theory at the End of the Century,* ed. Nicholas B. Dirks (Minneapolis: University of Minnesota Press, 1998), 9.

37. A. L. Kroeber and Clyde Kluckhohn, *Culture: A Critical Review of Concepts and Definitions,* 47 vols., vol. 1, Papers of the Peabody Museum of American Archeology and Ethnology (Cambridge, MA: Harvard University Press, 1952); and Raymond Williams, *Culture and Society: 1780–1950* (New York: Columbia University Press, 1983).

38. Deborah Sontag, "Who Was Responsible for Elizabeth Shin?," *New York Times Magazine,* April 28, 2002, 57; Howard W. French, "Depression Simmers in Japan's Culture of Stoicism," *New York Times,* August 10, 2002, 3; "Global Teen Culture—Does It Exist?," *Brand Strategy,* January 2, 2003, 37; Robin Toner, "Foes of Abortion Push for Major Bills in Congress," *New York Times,* January 2, 2003, 1.

39. Marshall Sahlins, "Two or Three Things That I Know about Culture," *Journal of the Royal Anthropological Institute* 5, no. 3 (September 9, 1999): 399–421.

40. See Bill O'Reilly, *Culture Warrior* (New York: Broadway, 2006).

41. For an influential deployment of the idea of a "cultural Left," see Richard Rorty, *Achieving Our Country: Leftist Thought in Twentieth-Century America* (Cambridge, MA: Harvard University Press, 1998); and, for a more obvious exercise in scapegoating, Dinesh D'Souza, *The Enemy at Home: the Cultural Left and Its Responsibility for 9/11* (New York: Doubleday 2007).

42. "How did [a culture of death] come about? Many different factors have to be taken into account. In the background there is the profound crisis of culture, which generates skepticism in relation to the very foundations of knowledge and ethics, and which makes it increasingly difficult to grasp clearly the meaning of what man is, the meaning of his rights and his duties." Pope John Paul II, *Evangelium Vitae* (The Holy See, March 25, 1995), www.vatican.va/holy_father/john_paul_ii/encyclicals/documents/hf_jp-ii_enc_25031995_evangelium-vitae_en.html.

43. See Lawrence E. Harrison and Samuel Huntington, eds., *Culture Matters: How Values Shape Human Progress* (New York: Basic Books, 2001); Samuel Huntington, *The Clash of Civilizations and the Remaking of World Order,* new ed. (New York: Free Press, 2002) and *Who Are We? The Challenges to America's National Identity* (New York: Simon and Schuster, 2004); Thomas Sowell, *Race and Culture: A World View* (New York: Basic Books, 1994), *Migrations and Cultures: A World View* (New York: Basic Books, 1996), and *Conquests and Cultures: An International History* (New York: Basic Books, 1998).

44. For a journalistic survey of the right-wing ascendance of the concept of culture, see David Brooks, "Questions of Culture," *New York Times*, February 19, 2006, http://select.nytimes.com/2006/02/19/opinion/19brooks.html.

45. See Alice O'Connor, *Poverty Knowledge: Social Science, Social Policy, and the Poor in Twentieth-Century U.S. History* (Princeton: Princeton University Press, 2001) 75; Handler, *Critics against Culture*, 200–202.

46. As early as 1986, Michael Omi and Howard Winant identified the right-wing strategy of attempting to reverse the civil rights gains of the 1950s and 1960s by rearticulating concepts of racial equality to shear them of their more radical implications or even reverse their meaning. Thus, for example, the idea of "reverse racism," which echoed the fundamental principles of racial equality but turned any state involvement in racial justice into de facto racism; Michael Omi and Howard Winant, *Racial Formation in the United States from the 1960s to the 1980s* (New York: Routledge, 1986), 117, 120, 129.

47. Horowitz claims, for example, that conservative students are oppressed by having to witness anti-Bush political cartoons or hear such comments in class; see David Horowitz, "In Defense of Intellectual Diversity," *Chronicle of Higher Education*, February 13, 2004, B12, http://chronicle.com/free/v50/i23/23b01201.htm. For a good discussion of the way conservatives have turned liberal rhetoric into "Trojan horses" for the Right, see Stanley Fish's rebuttal to Horowitz: "'Intellectual Diversity': The Trojan Horse of a Dark Design," *Chronicle of Higher Education*, February 13, 2004, B13–14, http://chronicle.com/free/v50/i23/23b01301.htm.

48. Samuel Huntington, "The Clash of Civilizations?," *Foreign Affairs* 72, no. 3 (1993): 22–49.

49. Susan Wright, "The Politicization of 'Culture,'" *Anthropology Today* 14, no. 1 (1998): 11; Gill Seidel, "Culture, Nation, and 'Race' in the British and French New Right," in *The Ideology of the New Right*, ed. Ruth Levitas (Cambridge: Polity Press, 1986), 107–35.

50. O'Connor, *Poverty Knowledge*, 17.

51. Rorty, *Achieving Our Country*, 88. For a similar argument focusing on racial and ethnic "diversity" and identity, see Walter Benn Michaels, *The Trouble with Diversity: How We Learned to Love Identity and Ignore Inequality* (New York: Metropolitan Books, 2006).

52. For an honorable effort at intervening responsibly in public discourse from the perspective of anthropological knowledge, see Catherine Besteman and Hugh Gusterson, *Why America's Top Pundits Are Wrong* (Berkeley: University of California Press, 2005).

53. Peter J. Richerson and Robert Boyd, *Not by Genes Alone: How Culture Transformed Human Evolution* (Chicago: University of Chicago Press, 2005), 55.

54. Clifford Geertz, *The Interpretation of Cultures* (New York: Basic Books, 1973).

55. All nationalisms are of course not the same. Benedict Anderson characterizes as "linguistic nationalism" one specifically European form that emphasizes the boundaries of language group. Other kinds of nationalism, such as popular nationalism, emphasize such elements as culture and religion. Finally,

"official nationalism" also uses features of popular custom, but the ruling elites tend to differentiate themselves from the populace. See Benedict Anderson, "Western Nationalism and Eastern Nationalism: Is There a Difference That Matters?," *New Left Review* 9 (May/June 2001): 31–42.

56. See Thomas C. Holt, "The Political Uses of Alienation: W. E. B. Du Bois on Politics, Race, and Culture, 1903–1940," *American Quarterly* 42, no. 2 (June 1990): 301–23; George Hutchinson, *The Harlem Renaissance in Black and White* (Cambridge, MA: Harvard University Press, 1995); and Arnold Rampersad, *The Art and Imagination of W. E. B. Du Bois* (New York: Schocken Books, 1990).

57. It is this sense of the malleability of the future that, I argue elsewhere, is at the heart of Boasian anthropology's modernism. See Hegeman, "Naïve Modernism and the Politics of Embarrassment," in *Disciplinarity and Practice: The (Ir)Resistibility of Theory,* ed. Stefan Herbrechter and Ivan Callus (Lewisburg, PA: Bucknell University Press, 2004), 154–77.

58. Jameson, *Singular Modernity,* 178.

59. Immanuel Wallerstein, "The National and the Universal: Can There Be Such a Thing as World Culture?," in *Culture, Globalization, and the World System,* ed. Anthony D. King (Minnesota: University of Minnesota Press, 1997) 97.

CHAPTER 1

1. James Clifford, *The Predicament of Culture: Twentieth-Century Ethnography, Literature, and Art* (Cambridge, MA: Harvard University Press, 1988), 95.

2. See Robert Brightman, "Forget Culture: Replacement, Transcendence, Relexification," *Cultural Anthropology* 10, no. 4 (November 1995): 509–46; Marshall Sahlins, "Two or Three Things That I Know about Culture," *Journal of the Royal Anthropological Institute* 5, no. 3 (September 9, 1999): 399–421; and Christoph Brumann, "Writing for Culture: Why a Successful Concept Should Not Be Discarded," *Current Anthropology* 40, suppl. (February 1999): S1–S27.

3. See, for example, Regna Darnell, *Invisible Genealogies: A History of Americanist Anthropology* (Lincoln: University of Nebraska Press, 2001); and Ira Bashkow, Matti Bunzl, Richard Handler, Richard Orta, and Daniel Rosenblatt, "A New Boasian Anthropology: Theory for the 21st Century," *American Anthropologist* 106, no. 3 (2004): 433–34.

4. Renato Rosaldo, *Culture and Truth: The Remaking of Social Analysis* (Boston: Beacon Press, 1989), 30–32.

5. Arjun Appadurai, *Modernity at Large: Cultural Dimensions of Globalization* (Minneapolis: University of Minnesota Press, 1996), 12.

6. For examples, see ibid. and Brumann, "Writing for Culture," S2–S3.

7. Matti Bunzl sees this kind of particularist fastidiousness, in which no knowledge is produced because every generalization is in question, as leading to the absolute nominalism of the Borgesian map: "Starting with a desire to challenge all essentialisms and question all generalizations, the ethnographies of today are often simultaneous exercises in total deconstruction and absolute

empirical specificity." Matti Bunzl, "The Quest for Anthropological Relevance: Borgesian Maps and Epistemological Pitfalls," *American Anthropologist* 110, no. 1 (March 2008): 57. My thanks to Bunzl for sharing with me an early version of this paper.

8. Lila Abu-Lughod, "Writing against Culture," in *Recapturing Anthropology*, ed. Richard G. Fox (Santa Fe, NM: School of American Research Press, 1991), 147.

9. Ibid., 149–57.

10. Brumann, "Writing for Culture," S11; Sahlins also cites several examples of anthropological distress over ethnographic subjects' "invented traditions."

11. *Reflexivization* is Peter Whiteley's term in "Do 'Language Rights' Serve Indigenous Interests? Some Hopi and Other Queries," *American Anthropologist* 105, no. 4 (2003): 712.

12. For just two of the many excellent studies of these processes, see Molly H. Mullin, *Culture in the Marketplace: Gender, Art, and Value in the American Southwest* (Durham: Duke University Press, 2001); and Michael F. Brown, *Who Owns Native Culture?* (Cambridge, MA: Harvard University Press, 2003).

13. Claude Lévi-Strauss, *Tristes Tropiques*, trans. John Weightman and Doreen Weightman (New York: Atheneum, 1973).

14. This desire for a space of exteriority to the marketplace is, I think, generally characteristic of the cultural turn. In cultural studies, it took its most characteristic form in the search for alternative cultures and subcultures that could be understood to be working outside the logic of commodity culture. The classic, if ultimately ambivalent, text of this work is Dick Hebdige, *Subculture: The Meaning of Style* (New York: Methuen, 1979).

15. Quoted in Annette B. Weiner, "Culture and Our Discontents," *American Anthropologist* 97 (1995): 18.

16. Adam Kuper, *Culture: The Anthropologist's Account* (Cambridge, MA: Harvard University Press, 1999), x. For another similar argument that culture is both "flabby" and "overspecialized," see Terry Eagleton, *The Idea of Culture* (Oxford: Blackwell, 2000), 36–37.

17. Kuper, *Culture*, x.

18. Ibid., xi.

19. Ibid.

20. Among the heavily disputed claims that Tooby and Cosmides portray as the common wisdom of the "Standard Social Scientific Model (SSSM)" are that a given human being belongs to one bounded culture; that culture is "accurately replicated from generation to generation"; that individuals are passive recipients of "culture," largely through the mechanism of the socialization of children; that the mind is a blank recipient of cultural content; that biological aspects of human behavior are insignificant; and that culture has little or no relationship to biological aspects of human existence. John Tooby and Leda Cosmides, "The Psychological Foundations of Culture," in *The Adapted Mind: Evolutionary Psychology and the Generation of Culture*, by Jerome H. Barkow, Cosmides and Tooby (New York: Oxford University Press, 1992), 31–32.

21. Ibid., 115–16.

22. Ibid., 116.

23. Social transmission remains for many animal behaviorists, evolution- ary biologists, and others a standard definition of "culture," which they see as a property shared by both humans and many animal species. For an inci- sive account of the significance of culture (as socially transmitted behavior) in human evolution, see Peter J. Richerson and Robert Boyd, *Not by Genes Alone: How Culture Transformed Human Evolution* (Chicago: University of Chicago Press, 2005).

24. Richerson and Boyd object to this ahistorical and speculative emphasis on the human hunter-gathering past by posing some straightforward questions: "But what about hunting and gathering? Couldn't we learn that as easily as we learn a language? Our lineage has lived as hunter-gatherers of some kind or another for the last two million or three million years. If we had to do so, couldn't we reinvent the things it takes to survive as a hunter-gatherer, in the same way that children reared in a multilingual community of immigrants are supposed to be able to invent a new language in a single generation? Good questions, but we think the answer is almost certainly 'Are you nuts?!'" (*Not by Genes*, 46).

25. Barbara Herrnstein Smith, "Super Natural Science: The Claims of Evolutionary Psychology," in *Scandalous Knowledge: Science, Truth, and the Human* (Durham: Duke University Press, 2006), 130–52.

26. Handler, "Cultural Theory in History Today," *American Historical Review* 107, no. 5 (2002): 1512–20, www.historycooperative.org/journals/ ahr/107.5/aho502001512.html, pars. 3–4.

27. Susan Hegeman, *Patterns for America: Modernism and the Concept of Culture* (Princeton: Princeton University Press, 1999), ch. 7.

28. My conception of totalization as a process of making connections is from Fredric Jameson, *Postmodernism; or, the Cultural Logic of Late Capitalism* (Durham: Duke University Press, 1991), 403; see also Jameson for a discus- sion of the difference between "totality" and "totalization," and postmodern anxieties about both (331–34).

29. Kuper, *Culture*, xi–xv.

30. See Virginia Dominguez, "The Messy Side of 'Cultural Politics,'" *South Atlantic Quarterly* 91, no. 1 (Winter 1992): 19–42; and Adam Kuper, *Culture: The Anthropologist's Account* (Cambridge, MA: Harvard University Press, 1999).

31. Walter Benn Michaels, *Our America: Nativism, Modernism, and Pluralism* (Durham: Duke University Press, 1995).

32. See Avery Gordon and Christopher Newfield, "White Philosophy," *Critical Inquiry* 20 (Summer 1994): 737–41.

33. Walter Benn Michaels, *The Shape of the Signifier* (Princeton: Princeton University Press, 2004); Steven Knapp and Walter Benn Michaels, "Against Theory," *Critical Inquiry* 8 (Summer 1982): 723–42; Steven Knapp and Walter Benn Michaels, "Against Theory 2: Hermeneutics and Deconstruction," *Critical Inquiry* 14 (Autumn 1987): 49–68. On Michaels's conception of intentional- ity, see also Jameson, *Postmodernism*, 212–17. My thanks to Robert Seguin for sharing with me his unpublished paper "The Spectre of the Universal, or, The Politicization of Walter Benn Michaels?," presented at the Eighth Annual

Conference of the Marxist Reading Group, University of Florida, Gainesville, March 31, 2006. Seguin both beautifully contextualizes Michaels's work and analyzes his political sympathies.

34. Alain Badiou, *Ethics: An Essay on the Understanding of Evil,* trans. Peter Hallward (New York: Verso, 2001), 18–29.

35. Michaels, *Our America,* 14.

36. Quoted in Verena Stolcke, "Talking Culture: New Boundaries, New Rhetorics of Exclusion in Europe," *Current Anthropology* 36, no. 1 (1995): 3.

37. Susan Wright, "The Politicization of 'Culture,'" *Anthropology Today* 14, no. 1 (1998): 10–11. Of course, I disagree with Wright's conclusion that this New Right rhetoric simply reinvented racism; I take much more seriously her point that rather they "appropriated the new ideas of 'culture' from cultural studies, anti-racism and to a lesser extent social anthropology, and engaged in a process of contesting and shifting meanings of 'culture,' 'nation,' 'race,' and 'difference'" (11). For a discussion of "right-wing Gramscianism" and its deployment of culture, see Gill Seidel, "Culture, Nation, and 'Race' in the British and French New Right," in *The Ideology of the New Right,* ed. Ruth Levitas (Cambridge: Polity Press, 1986), 107–35.

38. Stolcke, "Talking Culture," 4–9.

39. See George Yúdice, *The Expediency of Culture: Uses of Culture in the Global Era* (Durham: Duke University Press, 2003), 342.

40. Michaels, *Shape of the Signifier,* 10–11, 13; Jameson, *Postmodernism,* 181–217.

41. Walter Benn Michaels, "Plots against America: Neoliberalism and Antiracism," *American Literary History* 18, no. 2 (Summer 2006): 288–302; and see Michael Rothberg, "Against Zero-Sum Logic: A Response to Walter Benn Michaels," *American Literary History* 18, no. 2 (Summer 2006): 303–11.

42. Michaels, *Shape of the Signifier,* 16–17.

43. Eagleton, *Idea of Culture,* 38. Here Eagleton is echoing Samuel Huntington, who writes, "In class and ideological conflicts, the key question was 'Which side are you on?' and people could and did choose sides and change sides. In conflicts between civilizations, the question is 'What are you?' That is a given that cannot be changed. And as we know, from Bosnia to the Caucasus to the Sudan, the wrong answer to that question can mean a bullet in the head." Samuel P. Huntington, "The Clash of Civilizations?," *Foreign Affairs* 72, no. 3 (Summer 1993): 22.

44. Eagleton, *Idea of Culture,* 17.

45. Raymond Williams, *Culture and Society: 1780–1950* (New York: Columbia University Press, 1983); David Lloyd and Paul Thomas, *Culture and the State* (New York: Routledge, 1998).

46. Williams, *Culture and Society,* 126–29.

47. Williams, *Marxism and Literature* (New York: Oxford University Press, 1977), 20.

48. Karl Marx, *The German Ideology, Part I,* ed. C.J. Arthur (New York: International Publishers, 1986), 53.

49. Williams, *Marxism and Literature,* 19.

50. William Ray, *The Logic of Culture: Authority and Identity in the Modern Era* (New York: Blackwell, 2001), 7; italics in the original.

51. Richerson and Boyd, *Not by Genes Alone,* 11.

52. Herbert Marcuse, "The Affirmative Character of Culture," in *Negations: Essays in Critical Theory* (Boston: Beacon Press, 1968), 95.

53. Ibid., 103.

54. Ibid., 132.

55. T. S. Eliot, *Christianity and Culture* (New York: Harcourt Brace Jovanovich, 1988).

56. Slavoj Žižek, *The Puppet and the Dwarf: The Perverse Core of Christianity* (Cambridge, MA: MIT Press, 2003), 7.

57. There has been a strong strain of Protestant theology that equates culture with the fallen world. Indeed, evangelical engagement in the "culture wars" represents in many ways a significant shift from early twentieth-century evangelical views about believers' relationship to society. See H. Richard Niebuhr's classic *Christ and Culture* (1951; repr., New York: Harper Collins, 2001); George M. Marsden, *Fundamentalism and American Culture: The Shaping of Twentieth-Century Evangelicalism, 1870–1925* (New York: Oxford University Press, 1980); and Richard J. Mouw, *He Shines in All That's Fair: Culture and Common Grace* (Grand Rapids, MI: William B. Eerdmans, 2001).

58. Geoffrey H. Hartman, *The Fateful Question of Culture* (New York: Columbia University Press, 1997), 26. For another version of the idea of being haunted by culture, see Nicholas B. Dirks, "In Near Ruins: Cultural Theory at the End of the Century," in *In Near Ruins: Cultural Theory at the End of the Century,* ed. Nicholas B. Dirks (Minneapolis: University of Minnesota Press, 1998), 1–18.

59. Clifford, *Predicament of Culture,* 148.

60. Jacques Derrida, *Specters of Marx,* trans. Peggy Kamuf (New York: Routledge, 1994).

CHAPTER 2

1. Dwight Macdonald, "Masscult and Midcult," in *Against the American Grain: Essays on the Effects of Mass Culture* (New York: Da Capo Press, 1962), 3–75.

2. Serge Guilbaut, *How New York Stole the Idea of Modern Art: Abstract Expressionism, Freedom, and the Cold War,* trans. Arthur Goldhammer (Chicago: University of Chicago Press, 1983). Two exemplary challenges to Greenbergian orthodoxy are Andreas Huyssen, *After the Great Divide: Modernism, Mass Culture, Postmodernism* (Bloomington: Indiana University Press, 1986), 3–15; and Andrew Ross, *No Respect: Intellectuals and Popular Culture* (New York: Routledge, 1989), 42–64.

3. Fredric Jameson, *A Singular Modernity: Essay on the Ontology of the Present* (New York: Verso, 2002), 164. Numerous influential studies of modernism have subsequently challenged the idea of a division between modernism and other cultural forms. In this, Michael North's work is exemplary: *The Dialect of Modernism: Race, Language, and Twentieth Century Literature*

*(*New York: Oxford University Press, 1994), *Reading 1922: A Return to the Scene of the Modern* (New York: Oxford University Press, 1999), and *Camera Works: Photography and the Twentieth-Century Word* (New York: Oxford University Press, 2005).

4. Max Horkheimer and Theodor Adorno, *Dialectic of Enlightenment*, ed. Gunzelin Schmid Noerr, trans. Edmund Jephcott (Stanford: Stanford University Press, 2002), 25–27.

5. Frances Stonor Saunders, *The Cultural Cold War: The CIA and the World of Arts and Letters* (New York: New Press, 1999), 163, 234–78.

6. Dwight Macdonald, "A Theory of Mass Culture," in *Mass Culture: the Popular Arts in America*, ed. Bernard Rosenberg and David Manning White (Glencoe, IL: Free Press, 1957), 59–73.

7. John Fiske, *Reading the Popular*, new ed. (New York: Routledge, 1989), 2. Fiske would ultimately dismiss the entire idea of mass culture as a "contradiction in terms": "A homogeneous, externally produced culture cannot be sold ready-made to the masses: culture simply does not work like that. Nor do people behave or live like the masses, an aggregation of alienated, one-dimensional persons whose only consciousness is false, whose only relationship to the system that enslaves them is one of unwitting (if not willing) dupes. Popular culture is made by the people, not produced by the culture industry. All the culture industries can do is produce a repertoire of texts or cultural resources for the various formations of the people to use or reject in the ongoing process of producing their popular culture." John Fiske, *Understanding Popular Culture*, new ed. (New York: Routledge, 1989), 21–22; see also Andrew Ross and Patrick Brantlinger, *Bread and Circuses: Theories of Mass Culture as Social Decay* (Ithaca: Cornell University Press, 1983).

8. See Huyssen, *After the Great Divide*, 25–26.

9. Fredric Jameson, "Reification and Utopia in Mass Culture," *Social Text*, no. 1 (Winter 1979): 130–48; and Michael Denning, "The End of Mass Culture," *International Labor and Working-Class History*, no. 37 (Spring 1990): 4–18.

10. These dramatic postwar changes, frequently facilitated through direct government involvement, have been extensively discussed. See, for example, Lizabeth Cohen, *A Consumer's Republic: The Politics of Mass Consumption in Postwar America* (New York: Vintage Books, 2003); Robert Fishman, *Bourgeois Utopias: The Rise and Fall of Suburbia* (New York: Basic Books, 1987); Kenneth T. Jackson, *Crabgrass Frontier: The Suburbanization of the United States* (New York: Oxford University Press, 1985); and Elaine Tyler May, *Homeward Bound: American Families in the Cold War Era* (New York: Basic Books, 1988).

11. Stanley Walker, "Something to Remember You By," in *Mrs. Astor's Horse* (New York: Frederick A. Stokes, 1935), 22.

12. Ibid., 23–27.

13. Ibid., 26.

14. Nathanael West, "The Day of the Locust," in *The Complete Works of Nathanael West* (New York: Farrar, Straus, and Cudahy, 1957); William Carlos Williams, "The Crowd at the Ball Game," in *The Collected Poems of*

William Carlos Williams, vol. 1, *1909–39,* ed. A. Walton Litz and Christopher MacGowan (New York: New Directions, 1986–88), 233.

15. Frederick Lewis Allen, *Only Yesterday: An Informal History of the 1920s* (1931; repr., New York: Harper and Row, 1964), 54–57; H.L. Mencken, "In Memoriam: W.J.B," in *The Vintage H.L. Mencken,* ed. Alistair Cooke (New York: Vintage Books, 1955), 162–64.

16. Michael Warner, "The Mass Public and the Mass Subject," in *Publics and Counterpublics* (New York: Zone Books, 2002), 159–86.

17. Richard Sennett, *The Fall of Public Man* (New York: W.W. Norton, 1992), 299.

18. Gustave LeBon, *The Crowd* (1895; repr., New Brunswick, NJ: Transaction Publishers, 1997).

19. Raymond Williams, *Culture and Society: 1780–1950* (New York: Columbia University Press, 1983), 300.

20. Allen, *Only Yesterday,* 155–87.

21. See John B. Thompson, *The Media and Modernity: A Social Theory of the Media* (New York: Polity Press, 1995), 109.

22. See David Nasaw, *Going Out: The Rise and Fall of Public Amusements* (New York: Harper Collins, 1993); and Kathy Peiss, *Cheap Amusements: Working Women and Leisure in Turn-of-the-Century New York* (Philadelphia: Temple University Press, 1986).

23. See Sennett, *Fall of Public Man,* 12–16; and Marshall Berman, *All That Is Solid Melts into Air: The Experience of Modernity* (New York: Simon and Schuster, 1982), 287–348.

24. According to the *OED,* "mass culture" and some of its closer cognates, "mass audience" and "mass entertainment," all made their first print appearance in the early 1930s.

25. Anthony Rudel, *Hello, Everybody! The Dawn of American Radio* (New York: Harcourt, 2008), 159–75.

26. Edward J. Larson, *Summer for the Gods: The Scopes Trial and America's Continuing Debate over Science and Religion* (New York: Basic Books, 1997), 138–43.

27. John Kenneth Galbraith, *The Great Crash, 1929* (1954; repr., New York: Houghton Mifflin, 1997), 128–32.

28. Sue Collins, "Bonding with the Crowd: Silent Film Stars, Liveness, and the Public Sphere," in *Convergence Media History,* ed. Janet Staiger and Sabine Hake (New York: Routledge, 2009), 117–26.

29. Catherine Kerr, "Incorporating the Star: The Intersection of Business and Aesthetic Strategies in Early American Film," *Business History Review,* 64, no. 3 (Autumn 1990): 383–410; Collins, "Bonding with the Crowd"; Richard Abel, *Americanizing the Movies and "Movie-Mad" Audiences, 1910–14* (Berkeley: University of California Press, 2006), 247.

30. Alan Trachtenberg, *Lincoln's Smile and Other Enigmas* (New York: Hill and Wang, 2007), 5.

31. Quoted in ibid., 4.

32. Tom Gunning, "Phantom Images and Modern Manifestations: Spirit Photography, Magic Theater, Trick Films, and Photography's Uncanny," in

Fugitive Images: From Photography to Video, ed. Patrice Petro (Bloomington: Indiana University Press, 1995), 42–71.

33. See ibid.

34. For a more complete historical account of this transition in U.S. films, see Eileen Bowser, *The Transformation of Cinema, 1907–15* (Berkeley: University of California Press, 1994), 53–72.

35. Quoted in Bruce Lenthall, *Radio's America: The Great Depression and the Rise of Modern Mass Culture* (Chicago: University of Chicago Press, 2007), 4; and see Hadley Cantril, Hazel Gaudet, Herta Herzog, Howard Koch, and H. G. Wells, *The Invasion from Mars: A Study in the Psychology of Panic* (Princeton: Princeton University Press, 1940).

36. Cantril et al., *Invasion from Mars*, x.

37. See Lenthall, *Radio's America*.

38. See Rudel, *Hello Everybody!*

39. Theodor Adorno, *The Psychological Technique of Martin Luther Thomas' Radio Addresses* (Stanford: Stanford University Press, 2000), 1.

40. Ibid., 1–27.

41. David Jenemann, *Adorno in America* (Minneapolis: University of Minnesota Press, 2007), 1–46.

42. Theodor Adorno, *Current of Music: Elements of a Radio Theory*, ed. Robert Hullot Kentor (Cambridge: Polity Press, 2009).

43. Marshall McLuhan, *Understanding Media: The Extensions of Man*, 2nd ed. (New York: Signet, 1964), 259–68.

44. Quoted in Cohen, *Consumer's Republic*, 298.

45. On youth culture, markets, and moral panics, see Stanley Cohen, *Folk Devils and Moral Panics: The Creation of the Mods and the Rockers*, 3rd ed. (1972; repr., New York: Routledge, 2002), 149–72. On the complex relationship between market segmentation and the development of ethnic categories and identities, see Arlene Dávila, *Latinos, Inc.: The Marketing and Making of a People* (Berkeley: University of California Press, 2001); and Marilyn Halter, *Shopping for Identity: The Marketing of Ethnicity* (New York: Schocken Books, 2000).

46. Marshall McLuhan, "Introduction to the Second Edition," in McLuhan, *Understanding Media*, ix; and see Cecilia Tichi, *Electronic Hearth: Creating an American Television Culture* (New York: Oxford University Press, 1992), 3–9.

CHAPTER 3

1. Matthew Arnold, *Culture and Anarchy and Friendship's Garland*, vol. 6 of *The Works of Matthew Arnold* (New York: Macmillan, 1903).

2. Herbert Marcuse, "The Affirmative Character of Culture," in *Negations: Essays in Critical Theory* (Boston: Beacon Press, 1968), 96.

3. Ibid., 98.

4. Will Kymlicka, *Multicultural Odysseys: Navigating the New International Politics of Diversity* (New York: Oxford University Press, 2007), 28–31.

5. As Thomas Hill Schaub very usefully showed, this formalist aversion to context was shared by the New York Intellectuals, the other prominent group

of literary critics of the period, who are often seen as the liberal counterparts to the explicitly conservative New Critics; Thomas Hill Schaub, *American Fiction in the Cold War* (Madison: University of Wisconsin Press, 1991).

6. Michael Denning, *Culture in the Age of Three Worlds* (New York Verso, 2004).

7. Ibid., 3–10.

8. For an important discussion of 1989 as a significant historical punctuation point, see also Phillip E. Wegner, *Life between Two Deaths, 1989–2001: U.S. Culture in the Long Nineties* (Durham: Duke University Press, 2009).

9. See Susan Hegeman, *Patterns for America: Modernism and the Concept of Culture* (Princeton: Princeton University Press, 1999).

10. Raymond Williams, *Keywords: A Vocabulary of Culture and Society,* rev. ed. (New York: Oxford University Press, 1983), 11.

11. See Raymond Williams, *Culture and Society: 1780–1950* (New York: Columbia University Press, 1983).

12. Thomas C. Patterson, *A Social History of Anthropology in the United States* (New York: Berg, 2001), 107–9.

13. Psychological generalizations about national characters in the culture-and-personality style were rife throughout the policy documents of the postwar period. For example, George F. Kennan, one of the architects of the Marshall Plan, argued for restoring Germany's central position in the western European economy with the following language: "[Territorial] segregation and compression invariably arouses precisely the worst reactions in the German character. What the Germans need is not to be thrust violently in upon themselves, which only heightens their congenital irrealism and self-pity and defiant nationalism, but to be led out of their collective egocentrism and encouraged to see things in larger terms, to have interests elsewhere in Europe and elsewhere in the world, and to learn to think of themselves as world citizens and not just as Germans." George F. Kennan, "PPS/23: Review of Current Trends in U.S. Foreign Policy," in U.S. Department of State, Foreign Relations of the United States, *1948,* vol. 1, *General: United Nations,* pt. 2 (Washington, DC: U.S. Government Printing Office, 1976), 509–29, http://en.wikisource.org/wiki/Memo_PPS23_by_George_Kennan.

14. Guy Debord ruefully observed this relationship between culture, consumerism, and imperialism in *Society of the Spectacle* (Detroit: Black and Red Press, 1967), 193: "When culture becomes nothing more than a commodity, it must also become the star commodity of the spectacular society. Clark Kerr, one of the foremost ideologues of this tendency, has calculated that the complex process of production, distribution and consumption of knowledge already gets 29% of the yearly national product in the United States; and he predicts that in the second half of this century culture will be the driving force in the development of the economy, a role played by the automobile in the first half of this century, and by railroads in the second half of the previous century."

15. Richard E. Lee presents Williams as a transitional New Left figure between the donnish Leavisite mode of criticism of the liberal consensus and the fully institutionalized and theoretically elaborated cultural studies of the post-1968 generation. Richard E. Lee, *Life and Times of Cultural Studies: The*

Politics and Transformation of the Structures of Knowledge (Durham: Duke University Press, 2003), 35–69; see also Denning, who in *Culture in the Age* (77–78) describes Williams's *Culture and Society* in particular as a "vanishing mediator" in a tradition of liberal critique.

16. See Hegeman, *Patterns for America,* 159–64.

17. Kennan, "PPS/23," 13–14.

18. Quoted in Lourdes Arzipe, "The Intellectual History of Culture and Development Institutions," in *Culture and Public Action,* ed. Vijayendra Rao and Michael Walton (Stanford: Stanford University Press, 2004), 166.

19. They can be interestingly compared to Soviet counterparts like the Berlin House of Culture, which was dedicated to a more generalized European high culture. Of course, these differences also reflect the respective stereotypes of Russians and Americans common in Europe: if the Russians were cultureless because they were peasants, the Americans were cultureless because they had no native traditions. See Frances Stonor Saunders, *The Cultural Cold War: The CIA and the World of Arts and Letters* (New York: New Press, 1999), 18–21; Reinhold Wagnleitner, *Coca-Colonization and the Cold War,* trans. Diana M. Wolf (Chapel Hill: University of North Carolina Press, 1994), 128–49; and Serge Guilbaut, *How New York Stole the Idea of Modern Art: Abstract Expressionism, Freedom, and the Cold War,* trans. Arthur Goldhammer (Chicago: University of Chicago Press, 1983).

20. Oscar Lewis, *Five Families: Mexican Case Studies in the Culture of Poverty* (New York: Basic Books, 1959).

21. As Alice O'Connor shows in her outstanding history of the social science of poverty, both Frazier and Lewis were highly contradictory figures. The social democratic Frazier was a severe critic of both institutional racism and the political quiescence of the black bourgeoisie, yet he was also a consistent advocate of assimilation to both white and middle-class norms. Lewis, who also had leftist political leanings, both established a psychologization of poverty and insisted that the culture of poverty had its roots in the political economy of the "third world." In this sense both figures instantiate some of the contradictory political valences of the idea of a culture of poverty, which to many adherents suggested a need for radical transformation of the social order, yet, as O'Connor suggests, they "played into the liberal consensus by suggesting that the United States was no longer riven by the structural divides of class and race—and certainly not of gender—but faced a single, overarching problem of how to deal with the poor population in its midst." O'Connor, *Poverty Knowledge: Social Science, Social Policy, and the Poor in Twentieth-Century U.S. History* (Princeton: Princeton University Press, 2001), 80–83, 118–23.

22. Daniel Moynihan, *The Negro Family: The Case for National Action* (Washington, DC: U.S. Department of Labor, 1965), quoted in Charles A. Valentine, *Culture and Poverty* (Chicago: University of Chicago Press, 1968), 30.

23. See Michael Harrington, *The Other America: Poverty in the United States* (1962; repr., New York: Scribner, 1997). On the construction of poverty as an anomaly, see O'Connnor, *Poverty Knowledge,* 15.

24. See, for example, Susan E. Mayer, *What Money Can't Buy: Family Income and Children's Life Chances* (Cambridge, MA: Harvard University Press, 1998);

Orlando Patterson, "A Poverty of the Mind," *New York Times*, March 26, 2006, www.nytimes.com/2006/03/26/opinion/26patterson.html?ex=1179547200&en=c5988c201a1foofo&ei=5070; O'Connor, *Poverty Knowledge*.

25. The phrase is Sidney Hook's; quoted in Christopher Lasch, *The New Radicalism in America, 1889–1963: The Intellectual as Social Type* (New York: W. W. Norton, 1965), 306.

26. The term *antisystemic movement* was coined by Giovanni Arrighi, Terence Hopkins, and Immanuel Wallerstein as part of a challenge to a common assumption that popular political movements were either "social" or "national" in nature. They argued that in popular movements from the 1850s to the 1970s this distinction was overdrawn, in that both nationalist and social movements drew on strikingly similar rhetoric (especially of revolution and reform) and overlapped significantly so that nationalist movements contained strong social elements and social movements almost necessarily worked through their agendas in the context of national frames and ideologies. Immanuel Wallerstein, "Revolts against the System," *New Left Review* 18 (November/December 2002): 29–40; Giovanni Arrighi, Terence K. Hopkins, and Immanuel Wallerstein, *Antisystemic Movements* (New York: Verso, 1989).

27. Arrighi, Hopkins, and Wallerstein, *Antisystemic Movements*, 36.

28. No better example of this trend is Martin Luther King Jr., whose civil rights rhetoric increasingly turned from the issue of national justice to global concerns. This transition is evident in his famous final speech to the sanitation workers of Memphis, where he noted, "And also in the human rights revolution, if something isn't done, and in a hurry, to bring the colored peoples of the world out of their long years of poverty, their long years of hurt and neglect, the whole world is doomed." Martin Luther King Jr., "I See the Promised Land," www.mlkonline.net/promised.html; see also Martin Luther King Jr., "Beyond Vietnam," www.mlkonline.net/vietnam.html.

29. Antony Easthope, *British Post-Structuralism: Since 1968* (New York: Routledge, 1988), 33.

30. See Ross Benjamin, "Hostile Obituary for Derrida," *Nation*, November 24, 2004, www.thenation.com/doc/20041213/benjamin.

31. Jane Gallop, *Around 1981* (New York: Routledge, 1992), 3. As an example of Gallop's point, Toril Moi's groundbreaking *Sexual/Textual Politics* is structured around this very opposition between "Anglo-American feminist criticism" and "French feminist theory." Toril Moi, *Sexual/Textual Politics* (New York: Methuen, 1985).

32. Gallop, *Around 1981*.

33. Lee, *Life and Times*, 69.

34. Easthope, *British Post-Structuralism*, 16–22. Easthope writes that Althusser's work "is best regarded now as a structuralism passing over into post-structuralism" (21).

35. On the structuralism-culturalism debate, see Lee, *Life and Times*, 91–98. Culturalism was then, and remains, a term of rebuke in British critical circles. See David Lloyd and Paul Thomas, *Culture and the State* (New York: Routledge, 1998).

36. Dick Hebdige, *Subculture: The Meaning of Style* (New York: Methuen, 1979), 15.

37. Lynn Hunt, introduction to *The New Cultural History*, ed. Lynn Hunt (Berkeley: University of California Press, 1989), 1–22.

38. Ibid., 12.

39. Stephen Greenblatt, *Renaissance Self-Fashioning* (Chicago: University of Chicago Press, 1980) and "The Touch of the Real," in *The Fate of "Culture": Geertz and Beyond*, ed. Sherry B. Ortner (Berkeley: University of California Press, 1999).

40. Catherine Gallagher and Greenblatt are clear that the writing strategies of new historicism were in part in service of "a revival of the canon"; Gallagher and Greenblatt, *Practicing New Historicism* (Chicago: University of Chicago Press, 2000), 47–48.

41. Vincent P. Pecora, "Culture as Theater/Culture as Belief," *Criticism* 49, no. 4 (Fall 2007): 505–34. In a sense, new historicism served as an ideological rejoinder to the elements of 1960s radicalism that both Greenblatt and Geertz had, in their own ways, repudiated. On Geertz's political "right of center" positions during the student protests of the Vietnam era, see Adam Kuper, *Culture: The Anthropologist's Account* (Cambridge, MA: Harvard University Press, 1999), 130. Though Greenblatt has often professed an indebtedness to Marxist theory, his unease with radical theory and politics is strongly suggested in an often-quoted anecdote that Greenblatt himself relates, in which, in a course he taught on "Marxist aesthetics," an angry student demanded to know whether he was a "Bolshevik or a Menshevik" before slamming the door behind him. Greenblatt says the incident prompted him to stop teaching "Marxist aesthetics" in favor of courses with titles like "Cultural Poetics." Stephen Greenblatt, "Towards a Poetics of Culture," in *Learning to Curse: Essays in Early Modern Culture* (New York: Routledge, 1990), 147. See also Catherine Gallagher and Stephen Greenblatt, *Practicing New Historicism* (Chicago: University of Chicago Press, 2000), 9.

42. James Clifford, "Introduction: Partial Truths," in *Writing Culture: The Poetics and Politics of Ethnography*, ed. James Clifford and George E. Marcus (Berkeley: University of California Press, 1986), 4.

43. Gallop, *Around 1981*, 6.

44. See David Harvey, "Neoliberalism and the Restoration of Class Power," in *Spaces of Global Capitalism* (New York: Verso, 2006), 9–68.

45. See Masao Miyoshi, "'Globalization,' Culture, and the University," in *The Cultures of Globalization*, ed. Fredric Jameson and Masao Miyoshi (Durham: Duke University Press, 1998), 247–70. For an excellent discussion of the global dimensions of these issues, see Meghan Morris, "Humanities for Taxpayers: Some Problems," *New Literary History* 36, no. 1 (2005): 111–29.

46. Badiou's point is simple: medical ethics, when it enters into considerations of the cost of care, or cost to society, or whether one is a legal resident, represents a way of generalizing about "the sick" so as to obscure the singularity of the situation of care. He says, further, "A doctor is a doctor only if he deals with the situation according to the maximum possibility—to treat this person who demands treatment of him . . . as thoroughly as he can using everything

he knows and with all the means at his disposal, without taking anything else into consideration." Alain Badiou, *Ethics: An Essay on the Understanding of Evil,* trans. Peter Hallward (New York: Verso, 2001), 15.

47. For an insightful discussion of "transference" as the real dirty secret of the academy, see Elizabeth Freeman, "Monsters, Inc.: Notes on the Neoliberal Arts Education," *New Literary History* 36, no. 1 (Winter 2005): 83–95.

48. See Harvey, "Neoliberalism."

CHAPTER 4

A version of this chapter was published as "Culture, Patriotism, and the Habitus of a Discipline; or, What Happens to American Studies in a Moment of Globalization?," *Genre* 38, no. 4 (Winter 2005): 442–66. Portions are revised from "The 'Culture' of American Studies," *REAL (Yearbook of Research in English and American Literature)* 19 (2003): 47–63.

1. Jane Desmond and Virginia Dominguez, "Resituating American Studies in a Critical Internationalism," *American Quarterly* 48 (1996): 475–90; Carolyn Porter, "What We Know We Don't Know: Remapping American Literary Studies," *American Literary History* 6 (Fall 1994): 467–526; John Carlos Rowe, "Post-Nationalism, Globalism, and the New American Studies," *Cultural Critique* 40 (Fall 1998): 11–27; José David Saldívar, *Border Matters: Remapping American Cultural Studies* (Berkeley: University of California Press, 1997); and Priscilla Wald, "Minefields and Meeting Grounds: Transnational Analyses and American Studies," *American Literary History* 10 (Spring 1998): 199–218.

2. Alan Wolfe, "The Difference between Criticism and Hatred: Anti-American Studies," *New Republic,* February 10, 2003, 26.

3. Ibid.

4. Leo Marx, "On Recovering the 'Ur' Theory of American Studies," *American Literary History* 17 (Spring 2005) 121, originally published in *REAL: Yearbook of Research in English and American Literature* 19 (2003): 3–18.

5. Frances Stonor Saunders, *The Cultural Cold War: The CIA and the World of Arts and Letters* (New York: New Press, 2000); Michael Denning, *The Cultural Front* (New York: Verso, 1996).

6. In her reply to Marx, Amy Kaplan not only notes the irony of describing post–"Great Divide" scholars (many now in retirement) as upstart youngsters but cautions that in such narratives stereotyping and caricature operate all around; Kaplan, "A Call for a Truce," *American Literary History* 17 (Spring 2005): 141–47.

7. Simply among American communists, the National Question was a heavily debated topic, made particularly complex by a membership composed of immigrants from a diversity of countries. This complexity was only exacerbated in the context of struggles against European fascism and U.S. entry into World War II. See Paul Buhle, *Marxism in the United States* (New York: Verso, 1991), 121–33.

8. Buhle, *Marxism,* 155–83; and Caren Irr, *The Suburb of Dissent: Cultural Politics in the United States and Canada during the 1930s* (Durham: Duke University Press, 1998), 25–44.

9. For a discussion of F. O. Matthiessen as a central transitional figure between cultural nationalism and exceptionalism, see Irr, *Suburb of Dissent*, 25–44.

10. Certainly, black, Chicano, Puerto Rican, Native American, and other liberation movements used the language of nationalism for their causes, but this rhetoric was antithetical to that of U.S. nationalism. As one black antiwar slogan of the time, often attributed to Muhammad Ali, put it, "No Vietcong ever called me nigger."

11. Michael Bérubé, "The Loyalties of American Studies," *American Quarterly* 56, no. 2 (June 2004): 226.

12. Porter, "What We Know," 510.

13. See Michael Frisch, "Prismatics, Multivalence, and Other Riffs on the Millennial Moment: Presidential Address to the American Studies Association, 13 October 2000," *American Quarterly* 53, no. 2 (2001): 193–231.

14. Janice Radway, "What's in a Name? Presidential Address to the American Studies Association, 20 November 1998," *American Quarterly* 51, no. 1 (March 1999): 1–32. Nor was Radway unique in drawing this conclusion. See, for example, Gregory S. Jay, "The End of 'American' Literature," in *American Literature and the Culture Wars* (Ithaca: Cornell University Press, 1997).

15. See the discussion logs of the American Studies List (H-AMSTDY) for December 1998, archived on www.h-net.org/~amstdy/.

16. See Markku Henricksson, "1998 Seattle ASA Comments," ww.h-net .org/~amstdy/, and David Nye, "1998 Seattle ASA Comments," American Studies List (H-AMSTDY), www.h-net.org/~amstdy/; and for a different perspective, see André Kaenel, "Whence the Ire, What Are the Stakes, Where's the Beef? A Reply to David Nye," www.h-net.org/~amstdy/.

17. Michael Nichols, "1998 Seattle ASA Comments," www.h-net.org/~amstdy/.

18. Heinz Ickstadt, "American Studies in an Age of Globalization," *American Quarterly* 54, no. 4 (December 2002): 550.

19. Nye wrote, "A focus on ethnic and racial minorities might conceivably become the role of American Studies in the U.S., even if this would be a de facto surrender of much history, politics, and literature to other associations. But such a refocusing of American Studies would have quite a different meaning and effect outside the United States, where a university typically has only a handful of Americanists to cover all aspects of the U.S. The unstated assumption behind Radway's speech was that other departments at large American universities take care of history, literature, art, politics, environmental studies, and so on, and that American Studies ought to concentrate elsewhere." H-AMSTDY archive, posted December 7, 1998, www.h-net.org/~amstdy/.

20. Ickstadt, "American Studies," 551.

21. Fredric Jameson, "On 'Cultural Studies,'" *Social Text*, no. 34 (1993): 34.

22. Michael Hardt and Antonio Negri, *Empire* (Cambridge, MA: Harvard University Press, 2000), xiv.

23. David Harvey, *Spaces of Hope* (Berkeley: University of California Press, 2000), 68.

24. For Gramsci, Americanism centrally involved the encroachment after World War I of American methods of production—Fordism, Taylorism—but it also had utopian elements, signaling what Gramsci perceived as the lack in the United States of a feudal past. For other Europeans, however, Americanism also connoted cultural encroachments. See Antonio Gramsci, *Selections from the Prison Notebooks,* trans. Quintin Hoare and Geoffrey Nowell Smith (New York: International Publishers, 1971), 277–316.

25. See Sarika Chandra, *Dislocalism: The Crisis of Globalization and the Remobilizing of Americanism* (Columbus: Ohio State University Press, 2011).

26. Evan Watkins, *Throwaways: Work Culture and Consumer Education* (Stanford: Stanford University Press, 1993).

27. Sigmund Freud, *Civilization and Its Discontents,* trans. James Strachey (New York: Norton, 1962), 61.

28. Immanuel Wallerstein, "The National and the Universal: Can There Be Such a Thing as World Culture?," in *Culture, Globalization, and the World System,* ed. Anthony D. King (Minnesota: University of Minnesota Press, 1997), 93.

29. See Thomas L. Friedman, *The Lexus and the Olive Tree: Understanding Globalization* (New York: Anchor Books, 2000), 296–97; and for another discussion of the ideology of global homogenization, Phillip E. Wegner, "The Pretty Woman Goes Global: Or, Learning to Love 'Americanization' in *Notting Hill,*" *Genre* 38, no. 3 (Fall 2005): 309–26.

30. Kate Connolly, "Fast Coffee Bucks Viennese Tradition," *Guardian,* December 10, 2001, 16; and see Steven Erlanger, "An American Coffeehouse (or 4) in Vienna," *New York Times,* June 1, 2002, A1. The area around the Vienna Opera House is a hub for tourists and therefore hardly a pristine site of Viennese culture. It is perhaps relevant to this discussion of global culture and its circulations to note that when I visited it a few months after its opening, this particular Starbucks seemed to be patronized largely by Japanese tourists.

31. See Brian Larkin, "Indian Films and Nigerian Lovers: Media and the Creation of Parallel Modernities," in *The Anthropology of Globalization: A Reader,* ed. Jonathan Xavier Inda and Rosaldo Renato (Oxford: Blackwell, 2002); and Joan Gross, David McMurray, and Ted Swedenburg, "Arab Noise and Ramadan Nights: *Rai,* Rap, and Franco-Maghrebi Identities," in *The Anthropology of Globalization: A Reader,* ed. Jonathan Xavier Inda and Rosaldo Renato (Oxford: Blackwell, 2002).

32. Naomi Klein, "Reclaiming the Commons," *New Left Review* 9 (May/June 2001): 81–89.

33. Miranda Ewell and K. Oanh Ha, "Asian Immigrants Build Circuit Boards at Home in San Jose, Calif.," *San Jose Mercury News,* June 27, 1999; Miranda Ewell and K. Oanh Ha, "Asian Immigrants Exploited as Silicon Valley Electronics Contractors," *San Jose Mercury News,* June 28, 1999.

34. Peter Geschiere and Francis Nyamnjoh, "Capitalism and Autochthony: The Seesaw of Mobility and Belonging," *Public Culture* 12, no. 2 (2000): 423–52.

35. Hardt and Negri, *Empire,* 45.

36. Klein, "Reclaiming the Commons," 87.

CHAPTER 5

1. "Istanbul Rocked by Double Bombing," BBC News, November 20, 2003, http://news.bbc.co.uk/2/hi/europe/3222608.stm.

2. Charles Taylor, *A Secular Age* (Cambridge, MA: Harvard University Press, 2007); Giorgio Agamben, *The Time That Remains: A Commentary on the Letter to the Romans*, trans. Patricia Dailey (Stanford: Stanford University Press, 2005); Alain Badiou, *Saint Paul: The Foundation of Universalism*, trans. Ray Brassier (Stanford: Stanford University Press, 2003); Jean-Luc Nancy, *Dis-Enclosure: The Deconstruction of Christianity* (New York: Fordham University Press, 2008); Slavoj Žižek, *On Belief* (London: Routledge, 2001) and *The Puppet and the Dwarf: The Perverse Core of Christianity* (Cambridge, MA: MIT Press, 2003).

3. Richard Dawkins, *The God Delusion* (New York: Houghton Mifflin, 2006); Sam Harris, *The End of Faith: Religion, Terror, and the Future of Reason* (New York: W.W. Norton, 2004); Christopher Hitchens, *God Is Not Great: How Religion Poisons Everything* (New York: Twelve Books, 2007).

4. Pew Forum on Religion and Public Life, "Spirit and Power: A 10-Country Survey of Pentacostals," October 5, 2006, http://pewforum.org/surveys/pentecostal/; Jean Comaroff and John L. Comaroff, "Occult Economies and the Violence of Abstraction: Notes from the South African Postcolony," *American Ethnologist* 26, no. 2 (1999): 279–303; see also Mike Davis, *Planet of Slums* (New York: Verso, 2006), 194–98.

5. James Pinkerton, "Tuesday's Act Was Not about Nothing," *Newsday*, September 16, 2001, www.newamerica.net/publications/articles/2001/tuesdays_act_was_not_about_nothing.

6. The following discussion addresses the original article, Samuel Huntington, "The Clash of Civilizations?," *Foreign Affairs* 72, no. 3 (1993): 22–49, and the subsequent book, Samuel Huntington, *The Clash of Civilizations and the Remaking of World Order*, new ed. (New York: Free Press, 2002); see also Francis Fukuyama, "The End of History?," *National Interest*, no. 16 (Summer 1989): 3–18, and, for a discussion of Huntington as a response to Fukuyama, Tariq Ali, *The Clash of Fundamentalisms: Crusades, Jihads and Modernity* (New York: Verso, 2002), 272–73.

7. Huntington, "Clash of Civilizations?," 31.

8. Ibid., 25.

9. Huntington's understanding of Latin America as profoundly different from the "West" is made abundantly clear in his subsequent book, which sees Latin American immigration to the United States as a profound threat to "American" identity; Samuel Huntington, *Who Are We? The Challenges to America's National Identity* (New York: Simon and Schuster, 2004).

10. Huntington, "Clash of Civilizations?," 40.

11. Of course, the basic contours of Huntington's foreign policy views can be seen as going back much farther than the cold war. As Michael H. Hunt argues, "Like nineteenth-century advocates of Manifest Destiny faced by the perceived barbarism of Native Americans, Latin Americans, the Spanish, and the Chinese, [Huntington] posits U.S. civilizational superiority and on

that basis calls for a kind of moral rearmament to promote and defend Western values. In his construction, countries determined to find their own way are not part of a culturally diverse world, but wrong-headed rebels against a preponderant and enlightened West." Michael H. Hunt, "In the Wake of September 11: The Clash of What?," *Journal of American History* (September 2002): par. 4.

12. William James, *The Varieties of Religious Experience* (New York: Modern Library, 2002), 88–89.

13. Stanley Fish, "A Cartoon in 3 Dimensions; Our Faith in Letting It All Hang Out," *New York Times*, February 12, 2006.

14. See Stanley Fish, "Liberalism and Secularism: One and the Same," *New York Times*, September 2, 2007, http://fish.blogs.nytimes.com/2007/09/02/liberalism-and-secularism-one-and-the-same/.

15. Andrew Sullivan, "Leftism and Jihad II," February 13, 2006, http://andrewsullivan.theatlantic.com/the_daily_dish/2006/02/leftism_and_jih.html; Andrew Sullivan, "Quote of the Day II," February 13, 2006, http://andrewsullivan.theatlantic.com/the_daily_dish/2006/02/quote_of_the_da.html.

16. See Stanley Fish, *The Trouble with Principle* (Cambridge, MA: Harvard University Press, 1999).

17. Žižek, *Puppet and the Dwarf*, 7.

18. Ibid. Italics in the original.

19. "Calls Grow to Save Afghan Statues," CNN.com World, March 7, 2001, www.cnn.com/2001/WORLD/asiapcf/central/03/06/afghanistan.7/.

20. See Ussama Makdisi, "'Anti-Americanism' in the Arab World: An Interpretation of a Brief History," *Journal of American History* 89, no. 2 (September 2002), http://lp.hscl.ufl.edu/login?url=http://www.historycooperative.org//journals/jah/89.2/makdisi.html; and see Hunt, who comments, "The most remarkable feature of this nationalist upsurge [surrounding 9/11], for a historian at least, has been the ability of policy makers and most pundits to maintain a sense of injured innocence through an audacious repression of a half century of U.S. intervention in the Middle East" (par. 10).

21. Žižek, *Puppet and the Dwarf*, 6.

22. The classic study on this topic is Leon Festinger, Henry W. Riecken, and Stanley Schlachter, *When Prophecy Fails* (Minneapolis: University of Minnesota Press, 1956).

23. Group HSBC, *Business Connections: Your Guide to Business Culture around the World* (New York: Time Inc., 2002).

24. HSBC Group, "Fact Sheet," August 2008, www.hsbc.com.hk/1/PA_1_3_S5/content/about/about-hsbc/pdf/gfactsheet_aug08.pdf.

25. Edward Said rightly noted the "wish-fantasy" behind such role playing, which "depends on the rock-like foundations of European power"; Said, *Culture and Imperialism* (New York: Alfred A. Knopf, 1993), 160–61.

26. Emily S. Rosenberg, "Rescuing Women and Children," *Journal of American History* 89, no. 2 (September 2002): 456–65.

27. See Johannes Fabian, "Culture, Time, and the Object of Anthropology," in *Time and the Work of Anthropology: Critical Essays, 1971–1991* (Philadelphia: Harwood Academic Publishers, 1991).

28. Marshall Sahlins, "Two or Three Things That I Know about Culture," *Journal of the Royal Anthropological Institute* 5, no. 3 (September 9, 1999): 401.

29. Dipesh Chakrabarty, "Modernity and Ethnicity in India," in *Multicultural States: Rethinking Difference and Identity*, ed. David Bennett (London: Routledge, 1998), 91–110; and see Eugeen E. Roosens, *Creating Ethnicity: The Process of Ethnogenesis* (Newbury Park, CA: Sage Publications, 1989).

30. See Michael F. Brown, *Who Owns Native Culture?* (Cambridge, MA: Harvard University Press, 2003).

31. For a discussion of how a discourse of aboriginal cultural authenticity serves the interests of the Australian state, see Elizabeth A. Povinelli, *The Cunning of Recognition: Indigenous Alterities and the Making of Australian Multiculturalism* (Durham: Duke University Press, 2002).

32. Terence Turner, "Representing, Resisting, Rethinking: Historical Transformations of Kayapo Culture and Anthropological Consciousness," in *Colonial Situations: Essays on the Contextualization of Ethnographic Knowledge*, ed. George W. Stocking Jr. (Madison: University of Wisconsin Press, 1991), 285–313; see also Eva Marie Garroutte, *Real Indians: Identity and the Survival of Native America* (Berkeley: University of California Press, 2003); and Bruce Granville Miller, *Invisible Indigenes: The Politics of Nonrecognition* (Lincoln: University of Nebraska Press, 2003).

33. Georg Lukács, "'*Entäusserung*' ('Externalization') as the Central Philosophical Concept of *the Phenomenology of Mind*," in *Hegel and Contemporary Continental Philosophy*, ed. Dennis King Keenan (Albany: SUNY Press, 2004), 95–126.

34. Sahlins, "Two or Three Things," 401.

35. Richard Dawkins, "Why There Almost Certainly Is No God," *Huffington Post*, October 23, 2006, www.huffingtonpost.com/richard-dawkins/why-there-almost-certainl_b_32164.html?view=screen.

36. See also Taylor, *Secular Age*.

37. Michael Löwy and Robert Sayre, *Romanticism against the Tide of Modernity*, trans. Catherine Porter (Durham: Duke University Press, 2001).

38. Ibid., 230.

39. See ibid.

40. Žižek, *On Belief*, 113–22.

41. Ibid., 110.

42. Ibid., 127–28.

43. Ibid., 140.

44. It is in the idea of "unconditional engagement" that Žižek makes one of his most controversial moves, for the engagement (or rather, the commitment to actual freedom) of the born-again Christian is explicitly analogized to a Leninist understanding of commitment, to the extent that one is asked to be prepared to die for one's beliefs; *On Belief*, 1–5, 113–36.

45. Ibid., 148.

46. See also Slavoj Žižek, *Tarrying with the Negative: Kant, Hegel, and the Critique of Ideology* (Durham: Duke University Press, 1993), 200–237.

47. Slavoj Žižek, "Passion in the Era of Decaffeinated Belief," *Symptom* (Online Journal for Lacan.com), no. 5 (Winter 2004), www.lacan.com/passionf.htm.

48. See Richard Rorty, "On Ethnocentrism: A Reply to Clifford Geertz," *Michigan Quarterly Review* 25, no. 3 (1986): 525–34.

49. Fukuyama, "End of History?," 9.

50. Chakrabarty, in "Modernity and Ethnicity," reminds us that modernity is nothing if not a particular organization of time.

51. *Ofelas (Pathfinder)*, DVD, directed by Nils Gaup (Norway: Carolco Pictures [USA], 1987); *Himalaya*, DVD, directed by Éric Valli (France, Nepal: Kino International, 2000); *Atanarjuat*, DVD, directed by Zacharias Kunuk (Canada: Isuma, 2001); and *Ten Canoes*, DVD, directed by Rolf De Heer and Peter Djigirr (Australia: Palace Films, 2006).

52. For an account of how *Atanarjuat* addresses the legacy of *Nanook of the North*, see Michelle H. Raheja, "Reading Nanook's Smile: Visual Sovereignty, Indigenous Revisions of Ethnography, and *Atanarjuat (The Fast Runner)*," *American Quarterly* 59, no. 4 (December 2007): 1159–85.

53. *Ofelas* is set in 1000 AD; *Atanarjuat*, "at the dawn of the first millennium"; and *Ten Canoes* involves two historical moments: the relatively recent, but precontact, time of the frame tale, and the mythic Dreaming time of the central narrative. The historical dating of *Himalaya* is unspecified, but the pressbook and other material accompanying the film make clear that the Dolpopa people portrayed in the film live in an extremely isolated corner of Nepal from which tourists are barred entry. Igloolik Isuma Productions, "The Legend behind the Film," 2007, www.atanarjuat.com/legend/legend_film.php; Robert Lewis, "Making *Ten Canoes*," study guide, 2006, Australian Teachers of Media, Inc., 2; "*Himalaya* Pressbook," 1999, www.kino.com/himalaya/himalaya_download/himalaya_pressbook.pdf, 10.

54. Raheja, "Reading Nanook's Smile," 1166–67; for a discussion of indigenous uses of visual media, and debates surrounding their uses, see Faye D. Ginsburg, "Screen Memories: Resignifying the Traditional in Indigenous Media," in *Media Worlds: Anthropology on New Terrain*, ed. Faye D. Ginsburg, Lila Abu-Lughod, and Brian Larkin (Berkeley: University of California Press, 2002), 39–57.

55. *Ten Canoes;* Libby Tudball and Robert Lewis, "*Ten Canoes* Study Guide," 2006, Australian Teachers of Media, Inc., www.metromagazine.com.au/shop/downloads/sg310.pdf; Lewis, "Making *Ten Canoes*."

56. "Interview with Peter Djigirr," *Ten Canoes*, DVD, supplementary materials.

CHAPTER 6

1. See especially Charles Taylor, "The Politics of Recognition," in *Multiculturalism: Examining the Politics of Recognition*, ed. Amy Gutmann (Princeton: Princeton University Press, 1994); Will Kymlicka, *Liberalism, Community, and Culture* (New York: Oxford University Press, 1989) and *Multicultural*

Citizenship: A Liberal Theory of Minority Rights (New York: Oxford University Press, 1995).

2. Karl Marx, "Economic and Philosophical Manuscripts," in *Early Writings* (New York: Vintage Books, 1975), 342.

3. See Matti Bunzl, "The Quest for Anthropological Relevance: Borgesian Maps and Epistemological Pitfalls," *American Anthropologist* 110, no. 1 (March 2008): 53–60; and for a similar argument in the field of political theory, see David Peritz, "Toward a Deliberative and Democratic Response to Multicultural Politics: Post-Rawlsian Reflections an Benhabib's *The Claims of Culture*," *Constellations* 11, no. 2 (2004): 266–90.

4. See Alice Echols, *Daring to Be Bad: Radical Feminism in America, 1967–75* (Minneapolis: University of Minnesota Press, 1989).

5. Saskia Sassen, *Territory, Authority, Rights: From Medieval to Global Assemblages*, updated ed. (Princeton: Princeton University Press, 2008), 292.

6. Will Kymlicka, *Multicultural Odysseys: Navigating the New International Politics of Diversity* (New York: Oxford University Press, 2007), 39.

7. Loretta Chao and Jason Leow, "Chinese Children in Ethnic Costume Came from Han Majority," *Wall Street Journal*, August 14, 2008, http://online.wsj.com/article_email/SB121866988423738751.html; UN Office of the High Commissioner for Human Rights, "International Covenant on Economic, Social, and Cultural Rights," ratified January 3, 1966, http://www2.ohchr.org/english/law/cescr.htm.

8. Elizabeth C. Economy and Adam Segal, "China's Olympic Nightmare: What the Games Mean for Beijing's Future," *Foreign Affairs* 87, no. 4 (July/August 2008): 47–56.

9. See Christian Joppke, "The Retreat of Multiculturalism in the Liberal State: Theory and Policy," *British Journal of Sociology* 55, no. 2 (2004): 237–57.

10. Susan Wright, "The Politicization of 'Culture,'" *Anthropology Today* 14, no. 1 (1998): 7–15.

11. Kymlicka, *Multicultural Odysseys*, 77–128; see also Verena Stolcke, "Talking Culture: New Boundaries, New Rhetorics of Exclusion in Europe," *Current Anthropology* 36, no. 1 (1995): 1–24.

12. Bruce Granville Miller, *Invisible Indigenes: The Politics of Nonrecognition* (Lincoln: University of Nebraska Press, 2003); "Crofters' Indigenous Rights Call," BBC News, March 25, 2007, http://news.bbc.co.uk/2/hi/uk_news/scotland/highlands_and_islands/6493015.stm.

13. Sassen, *Territory, Authority*; Chao and Leow, "Chinese Children."

14. Sassen discusses this example extensively (*Territory, Authority*, 176–221).

15. See Aihwa Ong, *Flexible Citizenship: The Cultural Logics of Transnationality* (Durham: Duke University Press, 1999).

16. Sassen, *Territory, Authority*, 277–321; see also Seyla Benhabib, *The Claims of Culture: Equality and Diversity in the Global Era* (Princeton: Princeton University Press, 2002); and see David Jacobson, *Rights across Borders: Immigration and the Decline of Citizenship* (Baltimore: Johns Hopkins University Press, 1996).

17. See Bronislaw Szerszynski, "Local Landscapes and Global Belonging: Toward a Situated Citizenship of the Environment," in *Environmental*

Citizenship, ed. Andrew Dobson and Derek Bell (Cambridge, MA: MIT Press, 2006), 75–100.

18. Jesse Lee, "The White House Tribal Nations Conference," The White House Blog, November 5, 2009, www.whitehouse.gov/blog/2009/11/05/white-house-tribal-nations-conference.

19. Krissah Thompson, "U.S. Will Sign U.N. Declaration on Rights of Native People, Obama Tells Tribes," Washingtonpost.com, December 16, 2010, www.washingtonpost.com/wp-dyn/content/article/2010/12/16/AR2010121603136.html; United Nations, "United Nations Declaration on the Rights of Indigenous Peoples," September 13, 2007, www.un.org/esa/socdev/unpfii/en/drip.html.

20. Jillian Rayfield, "Latest Right-Wing Freak-Out: Obama Wants to Give Manhattan Back to Native Americans," TPM Muckraker, December 28, 2010, http://tpmmuckraker.talkingpointsmemo.com/2010/12/latest_right-wing_freak-out_obama_wants_to_give_ma.php?ref=fpblg.

21. United Nations, "The Universal Declaration of Human Rights," adopted December 10, 1948, www.un.org/Overview/rights.html; UN Office, "International Covenant."

22. Bruce Robbins and Elsa Stamatopoulou, "Reflections on Culture and Cultural Rights," *South Atlantic Quarterly* 103, no. 2/3 (Spring-Summer 2004): 429.

23. *Malama Makua v. Rumsfeld*, no. 00–00813, U.S. District Court of Hawaii, February 2, 2006; for an account of the context of this and other cases, see Kyle Kajihiro, "No Peace in Paradise: The Military Presence in the Hawaiian Islands," in *The Superferry Chronicles: Hawaii's Uprising against Militarism, Commercialism and the Desecration of the Earth*, ed. Koohan Paik and Jerry Mander (Kihei, HI: Koa Books, 2009), 272–83.

24. Kymlicka, *Liberalism, Community*.

25. See Jane K. Cowan, Marie-Bénédicte Dembour, and Richard A. Wilson, introduction to *Culture and Rights: Anthropological Perspectives*, ed. Jane K. Cowan, Marie-Bénédicte Dembour, and Richard A. Wilson (Cambridge: Cambridge University Press, 2001), 4–8.

26. Kymlicka, *Liberalism, Community*, 144; Susan Moller Okin, "Is Multiculturalism Bad for Women?," in *Is Multiculturalism Bad for Women?*, ed. Joshua Cohen, Matthew Howard, and Martha C. Nussbaum (Princeton: Princeton University Press, 1999); and see Anne Phillips, *Multiculturalism without Culture* (Princeton: Princeton University Press, 2007), in which the desire to defend multiculturalism and dispense with culture is more precisely a defense of "the rights of individuals rather than those of groups" (162).

27. See, for example, Jane K. Cowan, "Ambiguities of an Emancipatory Discourse: the Making of a Macedonian Minority in Greece," and David N. Gellner, "From Group Rights to Individual Rights and Back: Nepalese Struggles over Culture and Equality," both in Cowan, Dembour, and Wilson, *Culture and Rights*, 152–76 and 177–200 respectively.

28. For good overviews of these debates, see Kymlicka, *Liberalism, Community*; Cowan, Dembour, and Wilson, introduction; and Taylor, "Politics of Recognition" and the subsequent commentaries by various authors in Gutmann, *Multiculturalism*.

29. Kymlicka, *Liberalism, Community*, 177–78.

30. Okin, "Is Multiculturalism Bad." Though I am somewhat skeptical of her reliance on a Habermasian discursive model of politics, my position here is similar to that developed in Benhabib's *Claims of Culture*.

31. Sarah Harding, "Defining Traditional Knowledge—Lessons from Cultural Property," *Cardozo Journal of International and Comparative Law* 11 (Summer 2003): 512–13.

32. Ibid., 515–16.

33. Robbins and Stamatopoulou, "Reflections on Culture," 428.

34. See Simon Romero, "Rain Forest Tribe's Charge of Neglect Is Shrouded by Religion and Politics," *New York Times*, October 7, 2008, 6A; Kelly Hearn, "For Peru's Indians, Lawsuit against Big Oil Reflects a New Era; Outsiders and High-Tech Tools Help Document Firms' Impact," *Washington Post*, January 31, 2008, 14A; and Patrick Cunningham, "Amazon Indians Lead Battle against Power Giant's Plan to Flood Rainforest," *Independent*, May 23, 2008, 32.

35. Michael F. Brown, *Who Owns Native Culture?* (Cambridge, MA: Harvard University Press, 2003), 7–8. There is wide disagreement about the implications of protecting these kinds of intangibles within existing legal frameworks, especially those of intellectual property. For good overviews, see Shubha Ghosh, "Reflections on the Traditional Knowledge Debate," *Cardozo Journal of International and Comparative Law* 11 (Summer 2003): 497–510; Michael H. Davis, "Some Realism about Indigenism," *Cardozo Journal of International and Comparative Law* 11 (Summer 2003): 815–30.

Index

COVER DESIGN
Sandy Drooker

TEXT
10/13 Sabon

COMPOSITOR
Toppan Best-set Premedia Limited

PRINTER AND BINDER
IBT Global